Oliver Drewes

Terrarium Animals

from A to Z

> Reptiles, Amphibians, Arachnids, Insects
> Extra: Profiles of Feeder Animals

Contents

Animal Groupings

All About Terrariums

Profiles of Terrarium Animals

Appendix

Animal Groupings

An extremely wide variety of animal species may be kept in terrariums. In the following chapter, you will find information about the classes, orders, and families to which these species belong and about their characteristics.

Shrimps, Crabs, and Relatives
Decapoda

The order Decapoda, with its suborder Reptantia, the **crawling crustaceans**, belongs to the class Crustacea (crustaceans). This class is estimated to contain more than 40,000 species, while the order numbers more than 8,000 species. The family Coenobitidae, the **land hermit crabs,** is found worldwide along tropical coasts. These animals live in discarded snail shells to conceal their unprotected, soft abdomens from enemies. After molting, they frequently search out new shells. The commercially available land hermit crabs of the genus *Coenobita* are peaceful creatures, and they can be a real pleasure to watch.

Scorpions
Scorpiones

The order Scorpiones includes more than 1,500 species, grouped in nine families. Along with ten other orders, it belongs to the class Arachnida (arachnids). Scorpions occur worldwide, but they are most commonly found in the tropics and subtropics. Only about 25 species are dangerous to humans. With more than 500 species, the **thick-tailed scorpions** (Buthidae) are the largest family. With an adult length of more than 8 inches (20 cm), the emperor scorpion (see page 20), a member of the family Scorpionidae, is one of the largest scorpions. The Scorpionidae are also known as the Old World scorpions because their range extends from Africa through southeastern Europe and Asia to Australia, but none are found in the New World.

A painted reed frog, typically seen asleep in the daytime.

Water Is Vital

For most frogs and toads, including this red-eyed tree frog, a water bowl and a high humidity level in the terrarium are indispensable; otherwise, these animals will quickly become dehydrated. Daily misting with water is highly recommended. Amphibians can absorb moisture through their skin, but many reptiles meet their need for fluids by licking up droplets of mist found on leaves or decorations.

Once considered a subfamily of the Scorpionidae, the Ischnuridae now rank as a separate family. The smallest scorpion family, with fewer than 20 species, is the Iuridae, or **hairy scorpions.** The reproductive behavior of scorpions is extremely interesting. In the mating ritual, which resembles a dance and sometimes lasts for hours, the male deposits a sperm capsule to a bare spot on the ground. The female takes it up in her genital opening. The young are born about 14 months later. They climb onto the mother's back independently or with her help and are carried there for the first few weeks, until they become independent.

Spiders
Araneae

> The green and black poison-dart frog owes its popularity to its attractive coloration.

The order Araneae belongs to the class Arachnida (arachnids). It is grouped into these suborders: the **true spiders** (Labidognatha), the **primitive spiders** (Mesothelae), and the **tarantulas and relatives** (Orthognatha). The **tarantulas** (family Theraphosidae), with more than 850 species, are represented on all five continents. Their German name, *Vogelspinnen*, or "bird-eating spiders," is derived from the Latin species name *Aranea avicularia* and has to do with a painting by Maria Sibylla Merian, dated 1705. Its subject is a spider in the process of overpowering a hummingbird.

Avis means "bird" in Latin. Female spiders molt annually, but males normally do not do so again after the puberty molt. When molting, tarantulas lie on their backs.

Leaf insects, which resemble leaves, succeed in fooling their enemies.

Do not let this alarm you. The simplest way to sex adult spiders is to observe their pedipalps. Those of a male have enlarged tips that contain structures used to transfer his sperm to the female's genital opening. In addition, most male tarantulas have proportionately longer legs. A tarantula can also be sexed by observing its shed skin. That of a female will have sperm storage sacs. In most species, mating can end in the death of the male, if the female has not been fed enough beforehand and the terrarium keeper fails to separate them quickly. The urticating (stinging) hairs on the abdomen of many American tarantulas (*Brachypelma* species) are a defensive tool. They are flicked at an attacker and cause uncomfortable itching on the skin or even an allergic reaction. The bites of all tarantulas are extremely painful, but most are not seriously dangerous to people. Species that are the exceptions are clearly stated within the species discussion. The largest member of this family is the Goliath tarantula, 10 cm in length. One of the most frequently kept

TIP

Socialization among Different Species

When different species are housed together, male-male competition, predator-prey relationships, varying climate requirements, different activity periods, the danger of hybridization, the introduction of diseases alien to the species, and the usually limited space in home aquariums entail a great risk of disease, injury, or even death for the terrarium occupants. If keeping terrarium animals turns into a "collecting mania," each species should be allowed to have its own terrarium.

species is the Mexican red-knee tarantula. Biologists at the University of Saarbrücken have made an extremely interesting discovery about the way spiders adhere to smooth surfaces. Spiders' legs end in hair-like, extremely thin structures with tufts of hair called scopulae. These pads enable the spider to be in such close contact with the surface beneath that the attraction of the molecules alone holds it in place. The force of attraction is strong enough to hold 160 times the spider's weight.

Mantids/Praying Mantids
Mantodea

The order of mantids and praying mantids, along with 25 other orders, belongs to the class Insecta. Some

2,300 species of mantids and praying mantids are known to exist. **Mantids,** members of the family Mantidae, have become known for their occasional sexual cannibalism. The remarkable thing is that half-eaten males are still capable of mating because the copulatory movements are controlled by the last abdominal segment. *Sphrodomantis* species are among the most widely sold mantids.

Tortoises are kept in outdoor terrariums in summer.

Stick and Leaf Insects
Phasmida

> **Mississippi map turtles need an aquatic terrarium.**

This order—the stick and leaf insects—contains the family Phyllidae, the **leaf insects**, and five families of stick insects, or walkingsticks. Not only are leaf insects disguised by their anatomical mimicry of leaves, but they also imitate, through their jerky method of locomotion, pieces of plants blowing in the wind. Most species are nocturnal and rely on their perfect camouflage in the daytime.

TIP

UV Light Prevents Rickets and Molting Problems
Diurnal reptiles need ultraviolet (UV) radiation. UVA is important for skin pigmentation and regeneration. Animals exposed to UVA light molt more frequently and easily.
UVB is necessary to the synthesis of Vitamin D_3 in the skin. The vitamin helps process the calcium ingested in the diet. A lack of it would result in rickets. It has not been conclusively proved that snakes need UV light, but it is recommended here for diurnal species as a precaution.

Flap-necked or common chameleons are lively animals that can bite quite hard.

The gold dust day gecko is a good choice for newcomers to the terrarium hobby.

Frogs and Toads
Anura

The order Anura (frogs and toads), along with the salamanders, belongs to the class Amphibia (amphibians). It is subdivided into the suborders Archaebatrachia, **ancient or primitive frogs,** and Neobatrachia, **modern or advanced frogs,** and it contains almost 30 families, with a total of roughly 2,600 species.
Poison-dart frogs, Dendrobatidae, live in the tropical regions of South and Central America. They are also known as poison-arrow, dart-poison, and poison frogs. The poison protects them against predators and serves as a defense against microorganisms and fungi, which might attack their skin. Only a tiny number of species are dangerous to humans. Poison-dart frogs kept in terrariums are less poisonous than those in the wild because they obtain the toxins from the foods they eat, such as toxic ants. For this reason, long-term captives or captive-raised specimens contain little, if any, toxins in their skin secretions. In the reproduction ritual, the males carry the tadpoles on their backs into the water. In some species, the first tadpoles release inhibitors into the water to obstruct the growth of their siblings. **True toads,** Bufonidae—with few exceptions—occur worldwide in the most diverse regions. Toads are predominantly ground-dwelling, nocturnal animals. **Narrowmouth or microhylid frogs**, Microhylidae, occur on all the continents except Europe and parts of America. In contrast to other frogs and toads, the

> **When threatened, the frilled lizard displays its neck frill.**

tadpoles breathe through an opening located on the mid-line of the ventral surface because the external nasal ~~ings~~ develop only ~~before~~ metamor- ~~range~~ of the ~~neodactylid~~ ~~ctylidae,~~ ... ~~erica~~

~~aman-~~
~~lass~~
~~ans).~~
~~amanders~~
~~uborder~~

America. A friendly appearance, created by the broad mouth, and large eyes contribute to the popularity of the nocturnal species as terrarium animals. Most species of the family Hyper-oliidae, known as the **African tree frogs,** are small, arboreal frogs. Their range of distribution includes Africa, Madagascar, and the Seychelles. The **Old World tree frogs,** which belong to

Green basilisks are good runners, climbers, and swimmers.

the family Rhacophoridae, are found from Southeast Asia to Africa. Many Old World tree frogs lay their eggs in foam nests near bodies of water. **Fire-bellied toads,** which constitute the family Bombinatoridae, inhabit regions of Europe and Asia. These animals use their forelimbs along with their jaws to grasp their prey because they are unable to extend their tongues. Members of the family Pipidae, the **tongueless frogs,** spend their entire lives in the water. Like fish, they are equipped with a lateral line organ, with which they can measure pressure fluctuations in the water.

Salamanders
Urodela (Caudata)

The order Urodela (saladers) belongs to the Amphibia (amphib It includes the sal and their allies (

Green lizards can reach an age of more than 10 years.

Salamandroidea) and the **hellbenders and hynobiids** (suborder Cryptobranchoidea). The former group contains about 400 species in five families. **Salamanders and newts** (Salamandridae) occur in the northern hemisphere and are usually nocturnal, dark in color, and quite shy. In addition, there are some beautifully colored and diurnal species. Many species are not good candidates for keeping in a home setting because they require cool conditions. **Lungless salamanders**, Plethodontidae, are found in the Americas and Europe. This family contains the largest number of species in the order.

Because they lack lungs, they are dependent on conducting respiration through the skin and the oral cavity. **Mole salamanders** (Ambystomatidae) are found from Canada to Mexico. One of the best known is the Mexican axolotl, which spends its entire life in its larval stage (neoteny).

Lizards and Snakes
Squamata

The order Squamata, scaled reptiles, belongs to the class

Ascertaining the Sex of Snakes
The sexes cannot be told apart at first glance. Among the distinguishing sexual characteristics: Males have a longer tail, and the tail base is broader because of the hemipenes sacs. Python and boa males have longer anal spurs (see page 26). Veterinarians use the following method: They insert a lubricated probe, pushing it gently as far as possible into the cloaca. It can be slid a greater distance into the male than into the female.

Reptilia, reptiles. It is divided into the suborder Sauria, known as **lizards**, with about 4,600 species in more than 20 families, and the suborder Serpentes, **snakes**, with about 3,000 species in 10 families. The range of the family Agamidae, known as **agamas**, extends from Europe through Asia to Australia. Most agamas have large heads and long tails. Many species have combs of long spines, bony facial ridges, and dewlaps of loose skin under the neck, which are used in intimidation and courtship displays. The range of the **chameleons**, members of the family Chamaeleonidae, extends from southern Europe through Africa to South Asia. They evolved from the Agamidae and adapted anatomically to life in trees.

Sleepy or pinecone lizards really do look like pinecones.

These animals are known for their ability to change color, their independently moving eyes, and their harpoon-like tongues. With more than 1,000 species, the Gekkonidae, or **geckos**, are a large family. These terrestrial and arboreal, largely nocturnal animals occur worldwide in warm regions. Most species live chiefly on a diet of insects, while many like to lick soft fruit and honey.

The range of the family Cordylidae, known as the **spinytail or girdled lizards**, is limited to Africa and

Eastern ribbon snakes get along well together.

Madagascar. These lizards are definitely sun worshippers, and in terrariums they require very bright lighting. **Wall lizards,** members of the family Lacertidae, prefer dry, warm regions and are widely distributed, especially in the Mediterranean countries. Like geckos, if disturbed or alarmed they can shed their tails to distract a potential predator. They are diurnal and lively terrarium inhabitants. All the European species, such as the green lizard, are protected. The diverse family Iguanidae, known as **iguanas,** also

TIP

Terrarium Location
Terrariums should not be located in high-traffic areas such as hallways. If the animals panic when observed from above, you should place the terrarium at eye level. For animals that prefer to stay in the shade, don't let the sun shine directly onto their quarters. That can also quickly overheat the terrarium. Unheated wet terrariums with species that like cooler conditions are not suitable for rooms with temperatures above 68°F (20°C).

includes the genera *Anolis* and *Basiliscus*. With the exceptions of Madagascar, the Fiji Islands, and the Tonga Islands, iguanas are found only in America. In anatomy and behavior, they resemble the Old World agamas. The various habitats range from seacoasts through rainforests and deserts to high mountains. Iguanas are diurnal, and, depending on the species, live on the ground or in trees. They are good runners, as well as good climbers and swimmers. The **night lizards,** members of the family Xantusiidae, live in trees and seldom grow longer than 23 cm. They are often confused with geckos. Their range includes North and Central America, as well as Cuba. In the subfamily Serpentes, or **snakes,** the **colubrids** (Colubridae), with more than 1,800 species, are the richest in species. With the exception of the Arctic regions and Australia, colubrids throughout the world have adapted to their habitats as terrestrial, arboreal, burrowing, or aquatic species. Colubrids must be fed more often than boas and pythons because they digest their food much more quickly. **Boas and pythons,** members of the family Boidae, on the other hand, need not be fed for several months after swallowing a large prey animal. They are not poisonous and kill their prey by suffocation or constriction. The two best-known of the four subfamilies, **boas** and **pythons,** come from South and Central America and from Africa, with a few exceptions. The range of the **whiptail lizards and their allies (tegus),** members of the family Teiidae, is restricted to the American continent, where they inhabit a wide variety of habitats, ranging from rainforests to savannahs. In the New World, they are, so to speak, the counterpart of the mon-

The tiger salamander, a popular land-dwelling species.

itor lizards in the Old World. The largely diurnal **skinks,** members of the family Scincidae, are found worldwide in warm regions. In many species, comb-like scales protect the ear openings so that no sand can get in. Some species have well-developed limbs, whereas the limbs of others are completely absent. Some **moni-** **tor lizards,** or Varanidae, make completely suitable terrarium animals because they do not grow as large as the water monitor, which can attain a length of up to 3 m. The smallest representative of this family, the short-tailed monitor, is just 20 cm long. In their range, which extends from Africa to Australia, monitor lizards

The Mexican red-knee tarantula defends itself by flicking hairs.

The huge emperor scorpion can be kept even by novices.

live predominantly near bodies of water.

Tortoises and Turtles
Testudines

The order Testudines belongs to the class Reptilia, the reptiles. The order is subdivided into the suborder Cryptodira, **common-necked or straight-necked turtles**, and Pleurodira, **side-necked turtles.** Common-necked turtles retract the head into the shell by bending the neck in a vertical S shape, whereas straight-necked turtles retract the head and neck by laying it to the side in an S shape. The order contains about 250 species in 13 families. **Tortoises,** Testudinidae, occur in southern Europe, Africa, Asia, and America. These plant eaters, or herbivores, need plenty of space to move about and, if kept outdoors, a shelter or hide box for protection when the weather is bad. **Mud and musk turtles,** Kinosternidae, are native only to North and South America. They are primarily carnivorous and are both land and fresh-water dwellers. Bataguridae (Geomydidae), **Old World freshwater turtles,** are found on every continent except Australia. They include the largest aquatic

---

TIP

Allergic Reactions
If you have a history of allergic reactions to insect stings or spider bites, be very careful when caring for venomous arachnids such as tarantulas and scorpions. Seek immediate medical attention if a sting or bite produces symptoms of an allergic response.

> **The Costa Rican zebra tarantula in a defensive position.**

turtles of all. Their powerful toes are webbed. The **pond and box turtles**, members of the family Emydidae, are most widely distributed in southern North America. They live in swamps, rivers, and coastal lagoons, both on land and in the water. The red-eared slider is certainly the best-known member of this family. When full grown, it measures more than 30 cm in length, and if irresponsibly released, it can have a negative effect on many native turtle populations. A good alternative for hobbyists is the common musk turtle, which reaches less than half the slider's size. The females of all turtle and tortoise species need suitable conditions for egg laying; otherwise, they may die of egg binding.

Legal Regulations

Loss of habitat and removal from the wild are the chief causes of the increasing endangerment of many animal and plant species. To ensure the survival of these animals and plants, many international and local laws have been enacted to regulate the capture, shipping and possession of endangered species. Failure to comply with them can result in confiscation, large fines, and, in many

> **Most baby green iguanas sold in pet stores have been raised on farms in Latin America where adults are popular food items.**

instances, jail sentences. The two best known of these laws are the Convention on International Trade in Endangered Species of Wild Fauna and Flora (CITES) and the United States Endangered Species Act.

CITES is a voluntary international agreement among governments to reg-

Like all other day geckos, this large Madagascar day gecko is a CITES II species.

ulate the international trade in species of wild animals and plants to ensure that such trade does not threaten their survival. CITES regulates the trade in both the living plants and animals themselves as well as products made from them, such as fur coats, exotic leather goods, and tourist curios. Depending on the degree of threat to a species' survival, it is placed in one of following three categories: Appendices I, II, and III, with Appendix I species being the most endangered.

CITES regulations do not apply to the shipment of listed animals and plants within a particular country. It is therefore of little concern to hobbyists wishing to purchase a listed terrarium animal. Animal or plant species legally imported or domestically propagated within the United States can be sold and shipped interstate without any problems. Permits would only have to be obtained if one is hoping to import or export a listed species.

The Endangered Species Act was established to protect threatened and endan-

---

TIP

Food Supplements
All reptiles need regular doses of vitamins and calcium. Juveniles in particular require calcium and phosphorous as dietary supplements to promote healthy bone growth; females need it for formation of the eggs, which in some cases are quite hard-shelled; and turtles use these minerals to strengthen the carapace. Many brands of vitamin and mineral supplements that are meant to be either added to the food or sprinkled on food items are available at most pet stores.

gered species of plants and animals as well as to conserve their ecosystems and to develop recovery plans whereby their populations will increase to the point where they can eventually be removed from the list. According to a species' level of endangerment, it is listed in one of three categories. These are Endangered, Threatened, and Candidates for listing. While most listed species are native to the United States, there are also a considerable number of non-native species protected by this act. Under the provisions of the Endangered Species Act it is illegal to harass, harm, hunt, shoot, wound, kill, trap, capture, collect, or ship interstate or internationally any endangered or threatened species unless such acts are exempted by a permit.

Like CITES, the Endangered Species Act does not affect the average hobbyist. There are no listed species included within this book, and protected species are almost never sold at pet stores or by animal dealers. However, hobbyists who intend to collect animals from the wild should totally familiarize themselves with the list of protected species and should under no circumstances, collect them or damage their environment.

Readers should be warned that several endangered species are being captive-bred here in the United States and sometimes offered for sale. The original stocks of these species were captured or imported prior to the speciesí listing. One that comes to mind is the beautiful San Francisco gartersnake, *Thamnophis sirtalis tetrataenia*. Although you are legally able to buy these animals from the breeders, you cannot take them across state lines without previously obtaining a permit from the United

Although a CITES II species, Mexican fireleg tarantulas are being captive-bred in large numbers.

States Fish and Wildlife Service (USFWS).

State and Local Laws

There are many state and local laws applying to wildlife. Some protect species that are threatened within these individual jurisdictions but not within their entire ranges, whereas others ban the importation of species deemed potentially hazardous if released into the environment. For example, Texas protects the Texas horned lizard, *Phrynosoma cornutum*, and bans the importation of freshwater stingrays and piranhas.

There are also numerous state, county, and city laws regulating the keeping of certain species within their boundaries. In many heavily populated counties and cities, the possession of venomous and giant snakes, and wildlife that are perceived as being potentially dangerous such as tarantulas and exotic wild mammals is forbidden without first having obtained a permit or taking a state-sanctioned educational course. It is each pet owner's responsibility to research these laws prior to obtaining any animal.

Specialized Terms
from A to Z

➤ **Abdomen**
Posterior section of the body.

➤ **Adult**
Sexually mature, full-grown.

➤ **Anal spurs**
Rudimentary bones of the hind legs and pelvis in boas and pythons. Sometimes visible on both sides of the cloaca.

➤ **Base of the tail**
Point at which the tail joins the body.

➤ **Cannibalistic**
Feeding on others of its own kind.

➤ **Chelicerae**
First pair of spiders' appendages, used to grasp, kill, and tear apart the prey and to bring it to the mouth.

➤ **Cloaca**
Opening for eliminating excrement as well as for depositing and receiving sperm and/or eggs.

➤ **Comb organ/Pectines**
Comb-like structures on the underside of scorpions' abdomens, though to be sensitive to touch and ground vibrations.

Concave
Curved like the inner surface of a sphere.

➤ **Cork branch**
Branched limbs of trees from which cork bark tubes are peeled.

➤ **Femoral pores**
Glands along the inner surface of lizards' thighs. They are especially pronounced in males during mating season.

➤ **Habitat**
Area or environment where a species normally lives or occurs.

➤ **Hemipenes**
Dual male reproductive organs in male lizards and snakes. Located in special internal sacs behind the cloaca (hemipenal sacs).

➤ **Juvenile**
Young animal that has not reached sexual maturity.

➤ **Meadow plankton**
Insects collected in the wild with a sweep net. The procedure is not unproblematic from the standpoint of species conservation law.

➤ **Metamorphosis**
Transformation of the larval form into an adult and sexually mature animal in species whose juvenile stages differ from the adult stage, such as salamanders.

➤ **Metasoma**
Last, highly mobile, tail-like part of the abdomen of scorpions; the stinger is located at its tip.

➤ **Neotenic**
Retaining larval characteristics in the sexually reproductive adult.

➤ **Nuptial pads**
Hard calluses on the forelimbs developed by male amphibians during mating season. They help the males hold on tight to the females, which are usually larger, until the eggs are inseminated.

➤ **Parthenogenesis**
Nonsexual reproduction without males, also known as virgin birth.

➤ **Postanal scales**
Scales located directly behind the cloaca.

➤ **Preanal pores**
Enlarged glands anterior to the cloaca, useful in sexing many lizard species.

➤ **Preanofemoral pores**
All the preanal and femoral pores together.

➤ **Rickets**
Disease resulting from a lack of calcium and/or Vitamin D_3, causing the bones and carapace of young reptiles to soften.

➤ **Semen sac/Spermatheca**
Part of the sexual organ of female spiders in which the semen of the male is stored.

➤ **Snout-to-vent length (SVL)**
Measurement of the length from the tip of the snout to the cloaca.

➤ **Succulents**
Plants capable of storing water in the stem, roots, or leaves.

➤ **Territorial**
Defending its territory against others of the same kind.

➤ **Total length (TL)**
Measurement for body length, beginning with the tip of the snout and ending at the tip of the tail.

➤ **UV light**
Ultraviolet light, component of natural sunlight, and, for many species, important in the formation of Vitamin D_3. Depending on wave length, divided into UVA, UVB, and UVC light. Diurnal terrarium animals need UVA to form pigment and regenerate skin. UVB is significant for the calcium metabolism of reptiles. UVC kills germs. Overly long or intense radiation with UV light causes skin and eye damage in terrarium animals as well as in humans. Do not look directly into the light of a UV-type bulb.

All About Terrariums

Depending on their specific habitat requirements, the various species need different types of terrariums. Here you will find helpful examples— suggestions for setting up five types of terrariums—as well as descriptions of the basic equipment you will need.

Dry Terrarium

The term *dry terrarium* is used as an umbrella term for all heated, dry terrariums. Depending on the decorations and plantings, they are broken down into four types: desert, steppe, savannah, and rock terrariums.

Temperature: Depending on the species, at least 77°F (25°C) in the daytime, under radiant lamps up to 122°F (50°C); at night, reduce the temperature by at least 14–18°F (8–10°C) to room temperature or lower. Do not heat under hiding places and cavities, which serve the animals as cool, damp retreats.

> The animals in a desert terrarium need lots of warmth and light.

TIP

Islands of Moisture
Even dry terrariums need a moist area. You can sink a shallow container in the bottom material, in which you keep the same substrate moister. The water can run off through a hole in the bottom, in order to avoid standing water. The bottom-most layer, which should always be kept moist, can also be dampened selectively through tubing.

Humidity: During the day, 60% at most; in the mornings, however, it can shoot up for a short period of time when you mist.

Lighting: Very bright.

Substrate: Sand or fine gravel; depending on the species, up to 12 inches (30 cm) deep. Including some loam will keep any holes that are dug from collapsing.

Decorations/Plantings: Put real plants in pots, far away from radiant heat sources.

➤ Decorate desert terrariums sparsely; per ⅗ square yards (½ square meter), use

SHOPPING LIST

- ✔ Heating cable, mats, or lamps
- ✔ Sand (rounded particles), depending on the species, mixed with loam or soil
- ✔ Cave as hiding place
- ✔ Branches, roots, cactus skeletons, grapevine
- ✔ Plants such as succulents, artificial plants
- ✔ Heat stone/rock to aid digestion
- ✔ Water bowl
- ✔ Container for moisture island

1–2 plants and one root or cactus skeleton.

➤ Steppe terrariums need slightly more decor; per ⅗ square yards (½ square meter), use 3–4 plants and 2–3 roots.

➤ Decorate savannah terrarium lavishly; per ⅗ square yards (½ square meter), use 3–4 robust plants such as *Sansevieria*, agave plants, and soft-spined cactus species, and 2–3 roots, pieces of wood,

The collared lizard likes to bask on rocks.

Giant whiteknee tarantulas don't like wet substrates.

or stones. For safety of animals and yourself, avoid sharp-spined cactus and prickly pears.

➤ Rock terrariums are taller than the types listed above. Rocks are the predominant decor feature. Make certain rock formations are stable.

Woodland Terrarium

The woodland terrarium can be temperate or tropical. In terms of its temperature and atmospheric humidity ranges, it falls between the dry terrarium and the rainforest terrarium categories. Depending on the species being housed, its moistness and density of furnishings will vary.
Temperature: About

SHOPPING LIST

✔ Humus or terrarium soil, expanding clay, aquarium filter medium (cotton wool), foam, or fiberglass window screening
✔ Dry moss or leaves to cover the bottom surface
✔ Stone slabs, cork bark, roots as hiding places
✔ Depending on the species, climbing branches
✔ Slabs of cork bark or slate as a rear wall
✔ Water dish
✔ Heating cable or mat
✔ Depending on the species, a misting bottle or mini-fogger

Woodland terrariums should be kept out of strong hot sun and be well ventillated.

The Right Substrate
Not every substrate is equally appropriate for every terrarium type, every species, or every size of animal. Coarse or sharp-edged substrate materials, for example, can injure the intestines of juveniles if ingested along with their food. In extreme cases, intestinal blockage can result in death. Peat-based terrarium soil or humus for wet terrariums will become dusty if kept too dry and can lead to respiratory infections or, in spiders, to suffocation if the respiratory organs are affected.

The Pueblan milk snake needs a semiwet or semidry terrarium.

68–86°F (20–30°C); depending on the species, it rises to about 95°F (35°C) in some places. Put the terrarium in a location that does not receive strong sun to keep it from getting too hot. During hot summer weather as well as in winter, when most of the species housed in a woodland terrarium require lower temperatures, place it in a cool room.

Atmospheric humidity: Depending on the species being housed, 50–70%. Mist daily.

Lighting: For species from dry regions, bright light; for those from wet regions, relatively subdued lighting.

Fire salamanders leave their hiding places when it rains.

Substrate: A layer of expandable clay to prevent standing water; on top of it, a moisture-retaining substrate made of commercially

> **In a rainforest terrarium, the atmospheric humidity is high.**

available terrarium soil or a mixture of soil, sand, and peat; in between a layer of foam, cotton wool, or fiberglass screening to keep the finer substrate from trickling down into the expandable clay stratum or the animals from digging into it. Cover with moss or leaves.

Decorations/Plantings: Plants such as ivy and ferns native to our latitudes, *Scindapsus* or *Epipremnum* species, and *Ficus pumila*.

Rainforest Terrarium

Other names for this type are tropical or jungle terrarium.

Temperature: Depending on the species, 68–86°F

TIP

Atmospheric Humidity
To keep the humidity level high, mist the terrarium several times a day with lukewarm water. Ultrasonic foggers that convert water to real fog are more convenient. Rain pumps can be controlled by a timer or a hygrometer. Easiest of all is a water portion, with a temperature 3.5°F (2°C) above that of the air. But provide enough ventilation to prevent fungal growths.

(20–30°C) in the daytime, except for basking islands. In these usually tall terrariums, there is a temperature differential of several degrees between the bottom and the upper region. At night, no more than 9°F (5°C) below the daytime temperature.

Atmospheric humidity: Depends on the species being housed, but should not be less than 70%.

Lighting: Bright at the top, less brightly lit toward the bottom because of the lush vegetation, which creates

The black and yellow poison frog: well camouflaged, easy to overlook.

shade. Depending on the species, combine spot lamps with basic lighting (see page 41).

Substrate: Moisture-retaining substrate such as peat/sphagnum mix or terrarium soil (don't use potting soil; it decays quickly). To prevent standing water, the substrate can be placed on top of a layer of expandable clay. Foam or fiberglass screening will prevent the finer substrate from trickling down into the expand-

Pieces of cork offer this goliath tarantula lots of hiding places.

able clay layer. The substrate can be covered with leaves, moss, and pieces of bark.

Decorations/Plantings: Many species need a large water dish. Grapevine or cork branches can serve as places to climb, while cocofiber mats with pockets for plants or tree fern panels can be used as a rear wall. The panels will become green over time, once the seeds they contain begin to germinate. Suitable plants include some orchid species, bromeliads, *Scindapsus/Epipremnun* species, or *Ficus pumila*. Terrariums for forest-edge species, such as *Ameiva ameiva*, should be less thickly planted.

SHOPPING LIST

For the land portion:
- ✔ Rear wall suitable for planting
- ✔ Climbing or creeping plants
- ✔ Spot lamp or heat lamp
- ✔ Peat slabs, sphagum moss, tree fern fiber as a substrate

For the water portion:
- ✔ Sand or gravel
- ✔ Aquarium heater
- ✔ Aquarium filter
- ✔ Aquarium siphon

Oriental fire-bellied toads are popular aquarium inhabitants.

TIP

Water Portion

The water level depends on the terrarium design and the requirements of the species being housed (see Profiles). For animals that bathe or swim, you need to take the body volume into account, so that the water does not overflow. For species that are sensitive to chlorine additives in tap water such as the axolotl, you will need the water preparation chemicals used in aquariums. Attach controllable heaters in clay tubes, hollow rocks, or cork tubes to keep the animals from getting burned.

The Malayan box turtle needs climbing aids in the water portion.

Aquatic Terrarium

Depending on the size of the water portion and the design of the land portion, aquatic terrariums are divided into two types: marsh terrariums (paludariums) and riverbank terrariums (ripariums). The lines between the two types are not clearly drawn.

Temperature: Depending on the species, 59–75°F (15–24°C) in unheated aquariums, 75–86°F (24–30°C) in heated aquariums.

Lighting: In marsh terrariums, more subdued lighting for frogs, toads, and salamanders. Spot lamp or heat lamp to dry and heat terrar-

Tomato frogs, which are energetic diggers, often can be observed in the daytime as well.

iums for lizards such as water agamas and basilisks or for snakes such as water colubrids.

37

Substrate: The land portion should be kept relatively moist for amphibians, but somewhat dry for reptiles.
Decorations/Plantings: In a riverbank terrarium for mud turtles or newts, depending on the size of the species or of the terrarium, the land portion can be replaced by a planted box, placed at the edge of the terrarium or in the center as an island. To help the animal get out of the water, place the transition to the land portion at a slant or arrange branches or pieces of bark so that they protrude into the water.
Special needs: A good filter is needed to clean the water

> Tortoises thrive in an outdoor enclosure.

TIP

Overwintering
Aquatic turtles overwinter in ponds at least 48 in. (120 cm) deep; in colder regions they are moved into the terrarium in winter. For lizards and amphibians, create a frost-free hill 3.2 feet (1 m) high, into which you stick tubes 16–20 in. (40–50 cm) long, with a diameter equal to the size of the animals. If climate is severe, your animals can be overwintered in an unheated basement or cool sunporch.

in an aquatic terrarium. If the animals produce large amounts of feces, ⅓ of the water has to be changed at least every week.

Outdoor Terrarium

We usually think of these as rather large enclosures, but relatively small cages made of wire gauze or bars are also suitable for temporary housing outdoors. They are broken down into various types:

➤ **Dry landscape** for year-round outdoor housing of temperate zone true toads

Some aquatic turtles can be overwintered in a pond.

and lizards and, depending on temperature requirements, for housing tortoises for half or part of each year.

➤ **Marsh landscape** for lizards, newts, fire-bellied toads, and true toads (year-round, depending on origin).

➤ **Pond landscape** for frogs and toads, salamanders, water snakes (make certain they cannot escape!), as well as pond and box turtles and water turtles (year-round,

Green lizards enjoy basking in elevated places that make good vantage points.

depending on origin).
Requirements for sunny and
shady places, hiding places,
and waterproof shelter vary,
depending on the species
being kept. Tortoises need, if
at all possible, a shelter that
is enclosed on three sides
and can be heated. Get the
animals used to eating in
the same spots. On sand
and gravel, the excrement of
species that produce large
amounts of feces is readily
visible and can easily be
swept up.

Special needs: Animals from
outdoor terrariums develop
faster and are larger, but
remain shyer in general.
Outdoor pens have to be
escape-proof, to keep the
animals from escaping, con-
tributing to the adulteration
of the local fauna, or intro-
ducing exotic diseases to the
native fauna. Similarly, out-

TIP

Heating Stones
In the wild, tropical reptiles
like to spend time on
stones heated to a temperature of 104°F (40°C) by the
sun. In terrariums, heating
stones permit such ther-
moregulation. Pet supply
stores offer a wide selection of shapes and colors.
Without adequate warmth,
many reptiles are unable to
function properly. However,
many reptile keepers have
lost animals to heat stones
that malfunction and overheat and think that heat
lamps are a better choice.

door enclosures must be
constructed so that enemies
such as raccoons, cats, or
crows cannot get in.

Technology for the Terrarium

Technology regulates the
light, temperature, and
humidity in a terrarium.
The more closely these climate factors correspond to
those of the animals' places
of geographic origin, the
more apt they will be to display their natural behavior
in all its variety.

**Horizontal branches
used as basking spots
have to be quite strong.**

The higher the fogger is positioned, the more attractive the effect.

In the proper lighting the animals' coloration can develop to its full splendor, and your specimens will be distinctly more active. As the basic terrarium lighting, use 15–40 watt fluorescent tubes. They have a long service life and a good light yield, and they consume little power. Fluorescent UV bulbs are also available. For insects, amphibians, and nocturnal animals, energy-saving lamps (10–20 watts) are sufficient. Depending on the species (see Profiles), you will need spot heat lamps.

High atmospheric humidity in the terrarium is important for many reptiles to prevent molting problems. Amphibians absorb all the moisture they need through their skin. For many species, higher humidity levels promote reproductive activity. As an alternative to

TIP

Temperature Control
A reliable way of regulating the temperature is important for proper living conditions, lowering the temperature at night, breeding, and incubating the eggs of temperature-sensitive species. Timers or time switches adjust the temperature in a very inexact fashion. Special temperature regulators for terrariums with photocells or digital programming raise or lower the temperature very precisely and prevent overheating caused by defective heat sources.

daily misting, the atmospheric humidity can be raised by means of a heated water portion, a fountain, a waterfall, an ultrasonic fogger, or a rain pump. By ventilating the terrarium, using the equipment for a limited time, or employing a humidistat with a sensor or a timer, you can prevent the climate from becoming too damp and keep mold from forming.

The temperature is important because the metabolisms of the animals profiled here function properly only in specific temperature ranges. The substrate is heated with heating mats or a cable, best placed under a portion of the terrarium, providing a heat gradient. Heat lamps or infrared lamps raise the air and substrate temperature. Ceramic black heat emitters get very hot and should be attached in protective holders. Otherwise, the animals can get burned quite easily (see previous page).

Feeder Animals

Apart from a few herbivores such as spiny-tailed lizards, green iguanas, desert iguanas, prehensile-tailed skinks, and tortoises, as well as many insect species, most terrarium animals live on live foods. A wide selection of these feeder animals can be purchased from pet supply stores.

Food that you catch yourself is always fresh and certainly is the most nutritious. It may be time-consuming, however, to find suitable places for catching the animals. One must also be certain that any collected insects are pesticide-free.

By breeding feeder animals yourself, you can raise the quality of your terrarium animals' diet by ensuring that it is well balanced. Pet stores and mail order companies have all the supplies and equipment you need to start breeding.

Female house crickets do not chirp.

Nutritional Boost for Feeder Insects
Before you feed your terrarium animals live insects that you have purchased from a pet supply store, you need to gut-load them for several days. Especially suitable for this purpose are field-cricket food now available in pet supply stores and dry dog food. Before using the feeder insects, enhance their food value by placing them in a plastic container, dusting them with powdered calcium, vitamins, minerals, and trace elements, and shaking the container.

It remains to be considered whether the cost of maintaining such rearing facilities is really worth it.

What Feeder Animals Are Available?

➤ *Drosophila* (see page 44, 4), houseflies, blowflies, and wax moths are very often fed to amphibians and small lizards.

➤ Members of the order Orthoptera, such as house crickets, field crickets, grasshoppers, and cockroaches, are the main diet of many species. House crickets are available in several different sizes, but adults chirp loudly. Grasshoppers grow quite large and are ideal for larger terrarium animals. Be certain that you

1 > **Jamaican field cricket**

2 > **Pinkie mice**

3 > **Cockroaches**

4 > *Drosophila*

5 > **Springtails**

do not use toxic grasshopper species, such as lubbers, as food animals. Cockroaches do not chirp at all and are long-lived. The commercially available species usually will not reproduce if they get loose in your home.

➤ Mealworms are fed primarily to spiders and scorpions. The mealworms' calcium-phosphorus ratio is unsuitable for reptiles.

➤ Springtails (5), earthworms, and grindal worms are ideal for amphibians and their larvae.

➤ *Zophobas* larvae (king mealworms or super worms) make good feeder animals for both reptiles and amphibians.

➤ Fish, crustaceans, and zooplankton have a high protein and mineral content and are easy to digest.

➤ The category of small mammals includes mice (2), rats, and hamsters. Larger terrarium animals are also fed guinea pigs and rabbits. Breeding small mammals is best done in laboratory cages. Keeping them outside your home is advisable because of the odor they cause. Small mammals such as mice or rats are also available in frozen form and in various sizes. If your terrarium animals have trouble getting used to prekilled feeder animals, it is a good idea to move the food around a bit with long tweezers.

Snakes react to scents and heat. Place prekilled feeder animals in a plastic bag and put them in warm water to warm them to approximately body temperature. When feeding live rodents, there is always the risk that the rodent will severely bite or injure your snake. By feeding prekilled rodents, this risk is avoided.

➤ Birds are fed primarily to large lizards and to boas and pythons. They usually have less food value than rodents, but they add variety to the diet and are often accepted by species that refuse rodents. Chicks are usually used.

Obtaining Your Terrarium Animals

Terrarium animals can be bought at local pet stores and pet expos or ordered from animal dealers. It is a good idea to have your terrarium set up and ready for its inhabitants before you buy any animals.

Profiles of Terrarium Animals

Two hundred of the most popular animals for home terrariums, alphabetically arranged according to their common names and described in individual profiles that include their characteristics, tips on keeping and care, and brief information on the families to which they belong.

Explanatory Notes

Common name: The most frequently used English name.

Scientific name: Multipart Latin name. The first term designates the genus, and the second, the species. If there is a third part, it denotes the subspecies.

Also: Additional common and scientific names (in some cases, incorrect versions) and/or now-obsolete scientific names that are still in use.

Characteristics: Total length (TL) and snout-to-vent length (SVL) in inches (centimeters). For tortoises and turtles, carapace length (CL); for frogs and spiders, body length. Tips on what to look for when trying to sex adult animals. To ascertain the sex of snakes, see page 15. Special technical terms are explained on pages 26 and 27.

Terrarium: Terrarium type (see also In Brief at right) and tips on appropriate living conditions for each species. Required terrarium size, measured in width × depth × height, and based on minimum humane

requirements. If not otherwise stated, the size is that needed for an adult pair. For each additional animal, add 15 to 20 percent to the area as a rule (for details, see individual profiles). Information on the needs of each species in terms of air and, if applicable, water temperature, atmospheric humidity, length of lighting periods, and, if required, UV radiation.

Keeping/Care: Information on keeping the sexes together. Data on the length and temperature of the hibernation period. Hibernation is generally not required unless you are planning on breeding the animals or you cannot provide adequate warmth and lighting during the winter months. Information on the toxicity and/or dangerousness of the species and what you need to keep in mind.

Diet: List of the types of foods commonly used.

Behavior: Information on the animals' behavior in their natural habitat and in the terrarium.

Similar needs: Other species with similar requirements when kept in captivity.

In Brief

A systematic classification of each species described in terms of its class, order, suborder, and family. Description of the range, the geographic region in which the animal normally lives. Under "Important," information on the toxicity and/or dangerousness of the species and the safety measures the terrarium keeper must take.

Information Boxes

At a glance, the most important facts about terrarium type, level of difficulty, period of activity, and habit (characteristic occurrence). The individual symbols and data:

➤ Terrarium type

 Dry terrarium (see page 30)

 Woodland terrarium (see page 32)

 Wet terrarium (see page 34)

 Aquatic terrarium (see page 37)

 Aquarium, corresponds to the data on the water portion for an aquatic terrarium

Outdoor enclosure (see page 39)

➤ Level of difficulty

1: Suitable for beginners.
2: Suitable for terrarium keepers with previous experience.
3: Reserved for experts.
!: Indicates toxicity and/or dangerousness. Please read with care the information under "Keeping/Care" and/or "Important" in the In Brief section.

➤ Activity

 Diurnal

 Nocturnal

 Crepuscular

If more than one symbol appears, the main activity period is placed first.

➤ Habit

 Tree dweller, arboreal

 Bush/shrub dweller

 Land/ground dweller, terrestrial

 Rock dweller

 Water dweller, aquatic

49

African Clawed Frog

Xenopus laevis

Terrarium type: 〰️
Level of difficulty: 1
Activity: ☽
Habit: 💧

Characteristics: SVL up to 4½ inches (11 cm). Females have 3 small lobes or appendages around the cloaca. Males are about ⅓ to ½ smaller; in mating season, they have black nuptial pads (see page 26) on the undersides of the fingers.

Terrarium: Aquarium. Recommended size for up to 6 adults: 32 × 17 × 16 inches (80 × 35 × 40 cm). Water level at least 8 inches (20 cm). Coarse gravel as substrate. Water temperature 68–82.5°F (20–28°C). Lighting: 10–12 hours.

Keeping/Care: Animals of roughly the same size get along well. Include robust aquatic plants both rooted and floating. Furnish with wooden roots as hiding places. Cover the aquarium to keep the frogs from escaping.

Diet: Mosquito larvae, crustaceans, and frozen foods. If overfed, the species becomes quickly overweight.

Behavior: These animals live exclusively in the water, come to the surface to get air, and enjoy digging in the substrate. This frog is tongueless, seizing its prey with its jaws or uses its forelegs to bring food items to its mouth.

IN BRIEF **Class:** *Amphibians* **Order:** *Frogs and toads*
Suborder: *Ancient or primitive frogs* **Family:** *Tongueless frogs*
Range: *Bodies of standing water in Central Africa*

African Fat-tailed Gecko

Hemitheconyx caudicinctus

Terrarium type: 🏕️
Level of difficulty: 1
Activity: 🌅 🌙
Habit: 〰️

Characteristics: TL 8⅜ inches (21 cm), SVL 12 cm. Males have bigger heads, more massive bodies, stronger coloring, and preanal pores (see page 27).

Terrarium: Woodland terrarium with substrate 2 inches (5 cm) deep, mixture of soil and sand or gravel, which may be covered with leaves. Provide shallow water bowl and cork or clay tubes as daytime retreats and hiding places. Once habituated, the geckos will leave them to search for food. Recommended terrarium size for housing an adult pair: 24 × 16 × 16 inches (60 × 40 × 40 cm). Temperature 82.5–86°F (28–30°C), at night 68–71.5°F (20–22°C), basking islands up to 95°F (35°C). Atmospheric humidity 50–70%. Lighting: 10 hours.

Keeping/Care: Keep as a pair or as a group with only one male. Mist lightly daily. Hibernation: 8–12 weeks at 71.5–75°F (22–24°C).

Diet: Crickets, grasshoppers, and newborn mice. Occasionally, honey or mashed fruit.

Behavior: Predominantly terrestrial; rarely they will climb slanting branches. In the first few hours after laying eggs, the females will jump up at potential enemies and bite them.

IN BRIEF **Class:** *Reptiles* **Order:** *Scaled reptiles* **Suborder:** *Lizards* **Family:** *Geckos* **Range:** *Senegal to Cameroon*

African House Snake

Lamprophis fuliginosus

Also: *Boaedon fuliginosus*, brown house snake

Characteristics: TL, depending on subspecies, 40 inches (100 cm), rarely longer. To ascertain sex, see page 15.

Terrarium type: 🌵
Level of difficulty: 1
Activity: ☼ ☽
Habit: ⬚

Terrarium: Savannah terrarium with daytime hiding places in the form of cork or clay tubes and hollowed-out areas under flat stones. Provide branches for climbing and a dish of drinking water. Recommended terrarium size for housing a pair of 100-cm-long specimens: 40 × 20 × 40 inches (100 × 50 × 100 cm). To keep a third specimen, increase the area by 20%. Air temperature 71.5–82.5°F (22–28°C), at night 64.5–71.5°F (18–22°C), basking islands 86°F (30°C). Atmospheric humidity 50–70%. Lighting: 10–12 hours.

Keeping/Care: Very compatible with one another. In winter, keep 7°F (4°C) cooler day and night, and light for 6 hours.

Diet: Mice, rats, and chicks. To prevent two snakes from attempts to swallow the same food item, separate them at feeding time.

Behavior: Mainly nocturnal but can also be seen in the daytime on occasion.

IN BRIEF **Class:** *Reptiles* **Order:** *Scaled reptiles* **Suborder:** *Snakes* **Family:** *Colubrids* **Range:** *Egypt to South Africa, western Senegal, isolated occurrences in Morocco, one subspecies on the Arabian peninsula*

African Rock Python

Python sebae

Also: African python, rock python

Characteristics: TL 200 inches (500 cm), rarely up to 320 inches (800 cm). To ascertain sex, see page 15.

Terrarium type:
Level of difficulty: 2
Activity:
Habit:

Terrarium: Woodland terrarium with strong branches for climbing. An elevated place to rest will be in frequent use. Provide large water pan and places to hide. Recommended terrarium size for adult animals up to 100 inches (250 cm) long: 150 × 50 × 80 inches (250 × 125 × 200 cm). Specimens longer than 100 inches (250 cm) need terrariums of up to 150 × 100 × 80 inches (375 × 250 × 200 cm). Air temperature 82.5–90°F (28–32°C), at night 75–79°F (24–26°C), water temperature 75–79°F (24–26°C), basking islands 95°F (35°C). Atmospheric humidity 60–70%. Lighting: 10–12 hours.

Keeping/Care: Best kept singly because of their large size. Avoid dampness. Hibernation: 8–12 weeks with temperature lowered by 7–11°F (4–6°C) but not required. Do not buy a small specimen of this snake unless you have the room for a terrarium large enough to house it as an adult.

Diet: Small mammals, rabbits, chicks, doves, chickens, and ducks.

Behavior: In the wild, hides during the daytime. When in a terrarium, defensive behavior is pronounced.

IN BRIEF **Class:** *Reptiles* **Order:** *Scaled reptiles*
Suborder: *Snakes* **Family:** *Boas and pythons*
Range: *Central Africa to southern edge of Sahara*

African Spiny-tailed Agama

Uromastyx acanthinurus

Also: African spinytail, Moroccan dab lizard, *Uromastyx acanthinura*
Characteristics: TL 18 inches (45 cm), SVL 11¼ inches (28 cm). Males reach a larger size and have more prominent femoral pores (see page 26).

Terrarium: Desert terrarium with substrate 6–12 inches (15–30 cm) deep. Recommended terrarium size for housing an adult pair: about 60 × 48 × 36 inches (150 × 120 × 90 cm). Mist terrarium 2–3 times a week. Temperature 81–86°F (27–30°C), at night 59–68°F (15–20°C), basking islands 104–113°F (40–45°C). Atmospheric humidity under 50–60%. Lighting: up to 14 hours. UV radiation required.

Keeping/Care: Best kept as pairs or trios. High temperatures are required for the functioning of the digestive system. Feed moderately to avoid obesity. Hibernation: 4 months at 53.5–64.5°F (12–18°C).

Diet: Chopped mixed vegetables and fruit, such as collard greens, romaine lettuce, yellow and green squash, alfalfa pellets, dried peas and lentils, and bird seed should also be provided.

Behavior: Likes to dig. Changes color in order to control body temperature.

Terrarium type:
Level of difficulty: 2
Activity:
Habit:

IN BRIEF   **Class:** *Reptiles* **Order:** *Scaled reptiles*
Suborder: *Lizards* **Family:** *Agamas* **Range:** *Northwestern Africa*

Amazon Whiptail

Ameiva ameiva

Also: Dwarf tegu, jungle runner

Characteristics: TL up to slightly more than 24 inches (60 cm), SVL 10⅝ inches (27 cm).

Terrarium type: 🌱
Level of difficulty: 2
Activity: ☀
Habit: 🔲

Terrarium: Rainforest with moist substrate, 4–6 inches (10–15 cm) deep. Provide hiding places under roots and pieces of cork. Advisable to put robust plant species in pots, as these animals are diggers. Recommended terrarium size for housing an adult pair: 80 × 40 × 32 inches (200 × 100 × 80 cm). Temperature 77–90°F (25–32°C), at night 68–71.5°F (20–22°C), basking islands 104–113°F (40–45°C). Atmospheric humidity 70–80%. Lighting: 12–14 hours. UV radiation required.

Keeping/Care: Keep as a single animal, because the sexes can be quite incompatible. Supply water by misting daily, but don't fail to include an additional water bowl.

Diet: House crickets, field crickets, grasshoppers, and baby mice. Occasionally, sweet, overripe fruit.

Behavior: Lively, agile ground dwellers, fond of digging. Lives in rainforest edges and light gaps.

IN BRIEF **Class:** *Reptiles* **Order:** *Scaled reptiles*
Suborder: *Lizards* **Family:** *Whiptail lizards and their allies*
Range: *Rainforests of northern South America and Amazonia*

Amur Ratsnake

Elaphe schrenckii

Characteristics: TL up to 62 inches (180 cm), rarely to 80 inches (200 cm). Male bigger and longer, with longer tail.

Terrarium type: 🔼🔼
Level of difficulty: 1
Activity: ☀️ ▨
Habit: ▨

Terrarium: Woodland terrarium with substrate 4–6 inches (10–15 cm) deep, so that the snake can dig itself in. Mist substrate every morning. Provide pan for bathing, climbing branches, and places to hide. Recommended terrarium size for housing an adult pair: 72 × 36 × 72 inches (180 × 90 × 180 cm). To keep a third specimen, increase area by 20%. Air temperature 71.5–77°F (22–25°C), at night 61–68°F (16–20°C), water temperature 64.5–71.5°F (18–22°C), basking islands 82.5°F (28°C). Atmospheric humidity 60–70%. Lighting: 12 hours, partly UV.

Keeping/Care: Very compatible with others of their kind and good for keeping in groups. Larger specimens are best kept singly. Hibernation of 4 months at 46.5–50°F (8–10°C).

Diet: Mice or rats, chicks, and eggs.

Behavior: Terrestrial, but also likes to climb. Alert, not very aggressive.

IN BRIEF **Class:** *Reptiles* **Order:** *Scaled reptiles* **Suborder:** *Snakes* **Family:** *Colubrids* **Range:** *Southeastern Siberia, Manchuria, Korea to northeastern China*

Argentine Horned Frog

Ceratophrys ornata

Characteristics: SVL up to 4¾ inches (12 cm). Males smaller, with darker-colored throats and nuptial pads on the inner thumbs.

Terrarium type: 🌿
Level of difficulty: 2
Activity: ☀
Habit:

Terrarium: Rainforest terrarium with large water dish. Soil substrate, about 2½ inches (6 cm) deep, kept slightly damp. Because of digging, plants do best in flower pots. Provide hiding places under cork bark, flat stones, and roots. Recommended terrarium size for one adult: 32 × 16 × 16 inches (80 × 40 × 40 cm). Air temperature 75–82.5°F (24–28°C), at night 68–71.5°F (20–22°C). Atmospheric humidity 80%. Lighting: 10–12 hours.

Keeping/Care: Keep singly because of aggressiveness and cannibalism. These frogs tend to become overweight quickly. Change substrate often, as they produce large amounts of feces. Ventilate terrarium well.

Diet: House crickets, cockroaches, grasshoppers, earthworms, baby mice and rats. Mineral supplementation is essential.

Behavior: Wait motionless to capture prey, either resting on the ground and camouflaged by their color or slightly buried in the substrate. They can inflict a painful bite.

IN BRIEF **Class:** *Amphibians* **Order:** *Frogs and toads*
Suborder: *Modern or advanced frogs* **Family:** *Neotropical or neodactylid frogs* **Range:** *Southern Brazil, Argentina, Paraguay, and Uruguay*

Arizona Mountain King Snake

Lampropeltis pyromelana pyromelana

Terrarium type: 🏔️
Level of difficulty: 1
Activity: ☀️ 🌙
Habit: 〰️

Characteristics: TL 40 inches (100 cm), rarely up to 44 inches (110 cm). To ascertain sex, see page 15.

Terrarium: Woodland terrarium with hiding places under stones and cork slabs and in cork tubes. Substrate: mixture of sand, loam, and soil. Provide water container. Recommended terrarium size for housing 1–2 adult specimens: 40 × 20 × 20 inches (100 × 50 × 50 cm). Air temperature 77–82.5°F (25–28°C), at night 64.5–68°F (18–20°C), basking islands 90°F (32°C). Atmospheric humidity 50–70%. Lighting: 12–14 hours.

Keeping/Care: Animals of equal size can be kept as a pair if well fed. Advisable to keep singly, however, because cannibalism can occur. Hibernation: 10–12 weeks at about 50–59°F (10–15°C) will stimulate reproduction.

Diet: Mice, rats, and lizards of appropriate size.

Behavior: Lives hidden in thin pine forests and rocky terrain. Its color pattern mimics the appearance of a poisonous coral snake.

IN BRIEF   Class: *Reptiles* **Order:** *Scaled reptiles*
Suborder: *Snakes* **Family:** *Colubrids* **Range:** *Western United States to northwestern Mexico*

Axolotl

Ambystoma mexicanum

Terrarium type: 〰️
Level of difficulty: 1
Activity: ☀️ 🌓
Habit: 💧

Characteristics: TL 12 inches (30 cm), SVL 5½ inches (14 cm). Males recognizable by enlarged skin folds near the cloaca, which swell during mating season.

Terrarium: Aquarium; substrate as fine-grained as possible. Provide hiding places and robust aquatic plants for spawning. Recommended aquarium size for housing an adult pair: 32 × 14 × 16 inches (80 × 35 × 40 cm). Temperature 64.5°F (18°C), fluctuations between 59 and 82.5°F (15 and 28°C) are tolerated, but 77°F (25°C) should not be exceeded over the long term. Lighting: 10–12 hours.

Keeping/Care: Keep animals of the same size as a pair or as a group. Do not combine with fish. Use a water treatment product if the tap water contains chlorine and chloramines. Ensure good water quality, water movement, and oxygen enrichment. Hibernation: 8–10 weeks at 46.5–50°F (8–10°C).

Diet: Fish, worms, and frozen foods.

Behavior: Neotenic, reproducing as gill-breathing larva.

IN BRIEF **Class:** *Amphibians* **Order:** *Salamanders* **Suborder:** *Salamanders and their allies* **Family:** *Mole salamanders* **Range:** *Lake Xochimilco near Mexico City*

Ball Python

Python regius

Also: royal python

Characteristics: TL up to 64 inches (160 cm), rarely to 80 inches (200 cm). To ascertain sex, see page 15.

Terrarium type: 🌲
Level of difficulty: 3
Activity: ☼ ☽
Habit: ▭

Terrarium: Woodland terrarium with strong climbing branches and large water pan. Recommended terrarium size for housing an adult pair up to 64 inches (160 cm) long: 64 × 32 × 48 inches (160 × 80 × 120 cm). For each additional specimen, add 20% to area. Air temperature 75–86°F (24–30°C), at night 64.5–71.5°F (18–22°C), water temperature 73.5°F (23°C), basking islands 83–100°F (34–38°C). Atmospheric humidity 60–85%. Lighting: 12 hours.

Keeping/Care: Keep as a pair or in groups with only one male. This snake lies a long time in one place, so avoid overly wet substrate. Wild-caught specimens often reluctant to feed. Buy captive-raised specimens.

Diet: Mice, rats, and chicks.

Behavior: Very peaceful species. Females brood their eggs during incubation (about 100 days). The name *ball python* refers to these animals' habit of rolling up into a ball if danger threatens.

IN BRIEF **Class:** *Reptiles* **Order:** *Scaled reptiles*
Suborder: *Snakes* **Family:** *Boas and pythons*
Range: *West Africa to central Africa*

Banded Water Snake

Nerodia fasciata fasciata

Characteristics: TL about 44 inches (110 cm). To ascertain sex, see page 15.

Terrarium: Woodland terrarium with larger water container. Provide hiding places and retreats. Recommended terrarium size for housing an adult pair: 56 × 24 × 20 inches (140 × 60 × 50 cm). Increase area by 20% for each additional specimen. Air temperature 68–79°F (20–26°C), at night 59–70°F (15–21°C), water temperature 71.5–75°F (22–24°C), basking islands 86°F (30°C). Atmospheric humidity 60%. Lighting: 12 hours, partly UV.

Keeping/Care: Keep singly, as a pair, or as a group. Separate animals when feeding to prevent biting. If the animals are less active and eat less in fall, lower the temperature to 50–59°F (10–15°C) until early February withhold food, and keep the lighting turned off. Overly wet substrate encourages skin diseases.

Diet: Fish and pieces of fish, nightcrawlers, and young mammals. These animals are not picky feeders.

Behavior: Excellent swimmer and diver. Some individuals can be quite aggressive and resent handling.

Terrarium type:
Level of difficulty: 1
Activity:
Habit:

IN BRIEF **Class:** *Reptiles* **Order:** *Scaled reptiles* **Suborder:** *Snakes* **Family:** *Colubrids* **Range:** *Central to southeastern United States*

Bearded Dragon

Pogona vitticeps

Characteristics: TL 22 inches (55 cm), SVL up to 12 inches (30 cm). Femoral and preanal pores (see pages 26, 27) enlarged in males during mating season.

Terrarium type: 🌵
Level of difficulty: 2
Activity: ☀️
Habit: 🔲

Terrarium: Desert terrarium with river sand 4–6 inches (10–15 cm) deep. Provide places to hide and climb, as well as to bask. Recommended terrarium size for housing an adult pair: 60 × 48 × 36 inches (150 × 120 × 90 cm). Add 15% more area for each additional female. Temperature 82.5–86°F (28–30°C), at night 64.5–68°F (18–20°C), basking islands 104–113°F (40–45°C). Atmospheric humidity 50–70%. Lighting: 12–14 hours. UV radiation required.

Keeping/Care: Keep as a pair or as a group with only one male. Hibernation: 3–4 months at 59–64.5°F (15–18°C).

Diet: Field crickets, house crickets, cockroaches, young mice and rats. Provide 25% vegetarian diet: chopped mixed greens, pieces of apple and pear, berries, mineral supplements.

Behavior: Likes to bask. Quickly becomes friendly.

Similar needs: Eastern bearded dragon (*Pogona barbata*), Rankin's dragon or dwarf bearded dragon (*Pogona henrylawsoni*)

IN BRIEF **Class:** *Reptiles* **Order:** *Scaled reptiles*
Suborder: *Lizards* **Family:** *Agamas* **Range:** *Eastern Australia*
Important: *Numerous color mutations have been developed by selective breeding*

Bibron's Thick-toed Gecko

Pachydactylus bibronii

Also: *Pachydactylus bibroni*, Bibron's gecko

Characteristics: TL 8 inches (20 cm), SVL 4½ inches (11 cm). Males have a wider head than females.

Terrarium type: 🌵
Level of difficulty: 1
Activity: ☀️ 🌙
Habit: ◣ 🌳

Terrarium: Dry terrarium with rough cork wall and branches for climbing. Provide hiding places under piles of stones and pieces of cork. Substrate: sand or sandy soil. Plants such as *Sansevieria*. Recommended terrarium size for housing an adult pair: 24 × 24 × 32 inches (60 × 60 × 80 cm). Temperature 79–86°F (26–30°C), at night 64.5–71.5°F (18–22°C), in some places 95°F (35°C). Atmospheric humidity 40–60%. Lighting: 10 hours.

Keeping/Care: Keep as a pair, since both males and females can have trouble getting along with each other. Mist every other day; the animals will lick up the drops.

Diet: Field crickets, house crickets, grasshoppers, cockroaches, and wax moths.

Behavior: Climbs a lot, but is also frequently terrestrial. Once habituated, the animals will show themselves in the daytime.

IN BRIEF **Class:** *Reptiles* **Order:** *Scaled reptiles* **Suborder:** *Lizards* **Family:** *Geckos* **Range:** *Southwestern to southern Africa*

Black and Yellow Poison Frog

Dendrobates leucomelas

Also: Yellow-banded poison frog, bumblebee poison-dart frog

Characteristics: SVL 1⅝ inches (4 cm). Males very slightly smaller, identifiable by trilling mating call or by larger discs on fingers.

Terrarium type:
Level of difficulty: 2
Activity:
Habit:

Terrarium: Rainforest terrarium with large water container. Substrate: peat slabs or humus-rich forest soil. Coconut shells are ideal places to hide or lay eggs. Recommended terrarium size for housing an adult pair: 20 × 16 × 20 inches (50 × 40 × 50 cm). Add 50% to area for a breeding group of up to 4 specimens. Temperature 79–86°F (26–30°C), at night 64.5–68°F (18–20°C), water temperature 75°F (24°C). Atmospheric humidity 75–90%, at night up to 100%. Lighting: 12–14 hours.

Keeping/Care: Keep as a pair or as a group with one male and 2–3 females—no more, since they are quite aggressive toward each other. Don't keep with *D. tinctorius* (see page 107) and *D. auratus* (see page 134) because crossbreeding can occur.

Diet: Fruit flies, houseflies, aphids, and wax moths and their larvae. Vitamins and mineral supplements on a regular basis.

Behavior: Likes to hide under leaves and branches.

IN BRIEF **Class:** *Amphibians* **Order:** *Frogs and toads* **Suborder:** *Modern or advanced frogs* **Family:** *Poison-dart frogs* **Range:** *Venezuela, Guyana, and Brazil*

Black Iguana

Ctenosaura similis

Characteristics: TL 48 inches (120 cm), rarely 60 inches (150 cm), SVL 20–22 inches (50–55 cm). Males longer and bigger, with dorsal crests.

Terrarium type: 🔼🔼
Level of difficulty: 1
Activity: ☀️
Habit: ⬇️

Terrarium: Dry or woodland terrarium with climbing branches and hiding places such as cork tubes or large roots on the ground. Substrate suitable for digging. Use of artificial plants advisable. Recommended terrarium size for housing an adult pair up to 48 inches (120 cm) long: 110 × 88 × 66 inches (275 × 220 × 165 cm). Temperature 77–86°F (25–30°C), at night 64.5–71.5°F (18–22°C), basking islands 104–113°F (40–45°C). Atmospheric humidity 50–70%, at night 80–90%. Bright lighting: 12 hours. UV radiation required.

Keeping/Care: Keep as a pair or as a group with one male.

Diet: As juveniles, insects; later, mainly leafy plants, sprouts, and herbs. Vegetables such as cucumbers, tomatoes, and summer squash. Rarely, fruits. Every few months, young mammals.

Behavior: Ground-dwelling species that also climbs. In the wild, found in both arid and extremely wet regions.

IN BRIEF **Class:** *Reptiles* **Order:** *Scaled reptiles* **Suborder:** *Lizards* **Family:** *Iguanas* **Range:** *Southern Mexico to Panama*

Black Ratsnake

Pantherophis o. obsoletus

Also: Elaphe obsoleta obsoleta
Characteristics: TL 64 inches (160 cm). To ascertain sex, see page 15.

Terrarium type:
Level of difficulty: 1
Activity:
Habit:

Terrarium: Woodland terrarium with climbing branches and hiding places on the ground. Provide bathing pan that corresponds to the snake's size. Recommended terrarium size for 1–2 adults: 64 × 32 × 64 inches (160 × 80 × 160 cm). Air temperature 71.5–82.5°F (22–28°C), at night 64.5–68°F (18–20°C), water temperature 64.5–71.5°F (18–22°C), basking islands 82.5–90°F (28–32°C). Atmospheric humidity 60–70%. Depending on origin, values may differ. Lighting: 12 hours, partly UV.

Keeping/Care: These snakes get along well together, but keep adult specimens singly because of their size. Hibernation: 8–12 weeks at 59–64.5°F (15–18°C), specimens of northern origin at 46.5–50°F (8–10°C).

Diet: Mice and rats, chicks, and eggs.

Behavior: In some cases also crepuscular and nocturnal. Found near bodies of water and wet areas as well as upland forests.

IN BRIEF   **Class:** *Reptiles* **Order:** *Scaled reptiles*
Suborder: *Snakes* **Family:** *Colubrids* **Range:** *Various subspecies from southeastern Canada, central and eastern United States to Texas*

Black-tailed Cribo

Drymarchon corais melanurus

Also: black-tailed indigo
Characteristics: TL 104 inches (260 cm), but usually stays smaller.

Terrarium type: ⬜
Level of difficulty: 2
Activity: ☀
Habit: 🔲

Terrarium: Moist woodland or rain-forest terrarium with hiding places under stones and cork slabs and in cork tubes. Furnish climbing branches and bathing pan. Recommended terrarium size for housing an adult pair: 120 × 51 × 80 inches (300 × 130 × 200 cm). Air temperature 77–82.5°F (25–28°C), at night 68–73.5°F (20–23°C), basking islands 90°F (32°C). Atmospheric humidity 50–60%. Lighting: 10–12 hours, partly UV.

Keeping/Care: Best kept singly because cannibalism may occur. Hibernation: 8–12 weeks at about 68°F (20°C), with lighting period reduced to 6 hours. Do not keep overly wet

Diet: Mice, rats, chicks, fish, and occasionally eggs.

Behavior: Predominantly ground-dwelling, but also climbs on low vegetation. When threatened, it vibrates the tip of its tail, making a noise like that of a rattlesnake. Easily provoked to bite.

IN BRIEF **Class:** *Reptiles* **Order:** *Scaled reptiles*
Suborder: *Snakes* **Family:** *Colubrids* **Range:** *Mexico, Central America to Ecuador, Colombia, and Venezuela*

Black Thai Scorpion

Heterometrus scaber

Also: *Chersonesometrus scaber*, Asian forest scorpion

Characteristics: TL about 4–4¾ inches (10–12 cm).

Terrarium type: 🔼🔼
Level of difficulty: 2 !
Activity: ☽
Habit: ⬇⬇

Terrarium: Moist woodland terrarium with hiding places under pieces of bark and flat stones. Substrate: sandy soil or woodland soil, 2–6 inches (5–15 cm) deep, covered with leaves and pieces of moss. Keep slightly damp, but avoid standing water. Supply shallow water dish or wet sponge placed in a shallow saucer. Recommended terrarium size for one adult: 16 × 12 × 8 inches (40 × 30 × 20 cm). Temperature 79–82.5°F (26–28°C), at night 68–75°F (20–24°C), basking islands up to 95°F (35°C). Atmospheric humidity 70–80%. Lighting: 8–10 hours.

Keeping/Care: Susceptible to mite infestation. Keep singly because of cannibalism. *Heterometrus* species are more aggressive than their African relatives of the genus *Pandinus*. Their sting is painful, but only slightly toxic.

Diet: Depending on size, house crickets, grasshoppers, cockroaches, mealworms, beetles, *Zophobas* larvae, and young mice.

Behavior: Lives in holes it has dug or taken over from other animals in the same habitat.

IN BRIEF **Class:** *Arachnids* **Order:** *Scorpions*
Suborder: *Neoscorpionina* **Family:** *Old World scorpions*
Range: *Southeast Asia, China to the Philippines*

Blue Spiny Lizard

Sceloporus cyanogenys

Also: *Sceloporus serrifer cyanogenys*
Characteristics: TL 14⅛ inches (36 cm), SVL 5⅝ inches (14 cm). Males more brightly colored, with tail thickened at its base and prominent femoral pores (see page 26).

Terrarium type: 🌵
Level of difficulty: 1
Activity: ☀️
Habit: 〰️ ⬛

Terrarium: Dry terrarium with rear wall that can be climbed, stable piles of stones, and roots under which the animals can hide as well. Substrate: mixture of loam with sand or gravel. Plant with succulents. Recommended terrarium size for housing an adult pair: 40 × 24 × 24 inches (100 × 60 × 60 cm). Temperature 86–95°F (30–35°C), at night 68°F (20°C), basking islands 113°F (45°C). Atmospheric humidity 50–60%, at night 80%. Bright lighting: 14 hours. UV radiation required.

Keeping/Care: Keep as a pair or as a group with only one male, as males are very territorial. Sufficient lighting and UV radiation important for development of colors.

Diet: House crickets, cockroaches, field crickets, grasshoppers, wax moths and their larvae, and baby mammals. Occasionally leaves and flowers. Supply mineral supplementation.

Behavior: Lives in rocky countryside. Live-bearing.

IN BRIEF **Class:** *Reptiles* **Order:** *Scaled reptiles*
Suborder: *Lizards* **Family:** *Iguanas* **Range:** *Southern Texas to Mexico*

Blue-tailed Skink

Mabuya quinquetaeniata

Also: African blue-tailed skink, five-striped Mabuya, rainbow (rock) skink

Terrarium type: 🌵
Level of difficulty: 1
Activity: ☀
Habit: 〰

Characteristics: TL up to 12 inches (30 cm), SVL up to 4 inches (10 cm). Males more brilliantly colored.

Terrarium: Dry terrarium with sandy substrate, kept damp in parts. Provide places to climb and to hide in the form of branches, stone slabs, and roots. Recommended terrarium size for housing an adult pair: 32 × 20 × 24 inches (80 × 50 × 60 cm). Temperature 77–86°F (25–30°C), at night 64.5–71.5°F (18–22°C), basking islands 95–104°F (35–40°C). Atmospheric humidity: 40–50%. Lighting: 12–14 hours. UV radiation required.

Keeping/Care: It is advisable to keep only captive-bred animals because they are less fearful and will not injure themselves running into the terrarium walls. Keep as a pair. Provide places for basking.

Diet: Grasshoppers, field crickets, house crickets, meadow plankton, and occasionally mealworms. Mineral supplements.

Behavior: Peaceful when among its own kind, but aggressive toward other lizards. Burrows into the substrate, but also enjoys climbing.

IN BRIEF **Class:** *Reptiles* **Order:** *Scaled reptiles* **Suborder:** *Lizards* **Family:** *Skinks* **Range:** *Northern to southern East Africa*

Blue-tailed Tree Lizard

Holaspis guentheri

Also: Eastern serrate-toed tree lizard

Characteristics: TL 4¾ inches (12 cm), SVL up to 2½ inches (6 cm). Males identifiable by larger femoral pores.

Terrarium type: 🏔️
Level of difficulty: 1
Activity: ☀️
Habit: 🌳

Terrarium: Semimoist woodland terrarium with many, primarily vertical, branches for climbing. Provide rear wall suitable for climbing and cork tubes as hiding places. Substrate: mixture of sand and soil. Recommended terrarium size for housing an adult pair: 16 × 16 × 24 inches (40 × 40 × 60 cm). Temperature 82.5–95°F (28–35°C), at night 64.5–71.5°F (18–22°C), basking islands 104–113°F (40–45°C). Atmospheric humidity 50–85%. Lighting: 10–12 hours. UV radiation required.

Keeping/Care: Keep as a pair or as a group with one male. Keep 50°F (10°C) cooler for 8–12 weeks in winter. Make sure these lively animals don't escape at feeding time.

Diet: Small field crickets, house crickets, cockroaches, mealworms, and wax moths and their larvae. Mineral supplements on a regular basis.

Behavior: Not only jumps unerringly from branch to branch in the tropical lowlands and coastal forests of its range but also has the ability to glide up to 98.4 feet (30 m).

IN BRIEF **Class:** *Reptiles* **Order:** *Scaled reptiles* **Suborder:** *Lizards* **Family:** *Wall lizards* **Range:** *Central Africa, Sierra Leone to Tanzania*

Boa Constrictor

Boa constrictor

Terrarium type:	⌂⌂
Level of difficulty:	1
Activity:	☼ ☾
Habit:	🌳 🌿

Characteristics: TL up to 120 inches (300 cm), rarely to 160 inches (400 cm). To ascertain sex, see page 15.

Terrarium: Woodland or rainforest terrarium with stable branches or a firmly anchored climbing tree, as adult specimens get quite heavy. Set up a large water container. Substrate: mixture of soil and sand. Recommended terrarium size for housing an adult pair 120 inches (300 cm) long: 120 × 60 × 80 inches (300 × 150 × 200 cm). Increase area by 20% for each additional specimen. Air temperature 71.5–82.5°F (22–28°C), at night 68–71.5°F (20–22°C), water temperature 77°F (25°C), basking islands 86–95°F (30–35°C). Atmospheric humidity 70–80%. Lighting: 12 hours.

Keeping/Care: Keep as a single specimen or in pairs. Adults require spacious quarters.

Diet: Depending on size, mice, rats, guinea pigs, rabbits, or poultry.

Behavior: With increasing age, they spend more time on the ground, but can also climb well. Various subspecies can be found in dry and rainforest areas.

IN BRIEF **Class:** *Reptiles* **Order:** *Scaled reptiles*
Suborder: *Snakes* **Family:** *Boas and pythons*
Range: *Central to South America*

Brazilian Black Tarantula

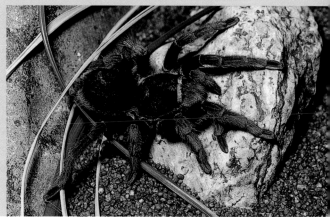

Grammostola pulchra

Characteristics: Body 2½–2⅞ inches (6–7 cm). Adult males have longer legs and enlarged pedipalp tips. See page 9 for additional sexing information.

Terrarium type: 🔲🔲
Level of difficulty: 1
Activity: 🔲 🌙
Habit: 🔲

Terrarium: Rainforest terrarium with substrate about 4 inches (10 cm) deep, slightly damp. Suitable materials: compressed humus made from coconut fiber or peat. Provide caves of cork bark with a diameter of about 6 inches (15 cm). Supply shallow water dish. Recommended terrarium size for one adult: 12 × 12 × 12 inches (30 × 30 × 30 cm). Temperature 81–91.5°F (27–33°C), at night 75–79°F (24–26°C). Atmospheric humidity 80%. Lighting: 8–10 hours.

Keeping/Care: Keep male or female singly. Maintaining the high atmospheric humidity levels is very important; otherwise, the tarantulas quickly become dehydrated.

Diet: Depending on size, flies, wax moths, house crickets, field crickets, cockroaches, small lizards, and baby mice.

Behavior: Peaceful species. Regularly digs up the terrarium soil and is often observed outside of its hiding place.

IN BRIEF   **Class:** *Arachnids* **Order:** *Spiders*
Suborder: *Tarantulas and relatives* **Family:** *Tarantulas*
Range: *Southwestern Brazil in the Rio Janeiro river basin northeast of Uruguay*

Brazilian Blue-green Pinktoe Tarantula

Avicularia geroldi

Also: blue and red pinktoe

Characteristics: Body up to 2¾ inches (7 cm). Males have enlarged pedipalp tips and longer legs. Easy to confuse with *Avicularia metallica* (see page 171), but has a less metallic sheen.

Terrarium: Rainforest terrarium with cork tube placed in upright position, cork branches, and back wall that can be climbed, possibly made of pressed cork. Substrate: leaf mold or coconut humus, which must always be kept damp but never wet. Provide water container. Recommended terrarium size for one adult specimen: 12 × 12 × 16 inches (30 × 30 × 40 cm). Temperature 75–82.5°F (24–28°C), at night 64.5–71.5°F (18–22°C). Atmospheric humidity 70–85%. Lighting: 8–10 hours.

Keeping/Care: Keep this species singly. Though first described only recently, in 1999, by Tesmoingt, it is already relatively easy to find commercially captive-raised young; this speaks for its suitability as a terrarium animal.

Diet: Flies, house crickets, field crickets, and baby mammals.

Behavior: Peaceful, nonaggressive tree dweller that can leap long distances.

Terrarium type:
Level of difficulty: 1
Activity:
Habit:

IN BRIEF **Class:** *Arachnids* **Order:** *Spiders*
Suborder: *Tarantulas and relatives* **Family:** *Tarantulas*
Range: *Venezuela, northern Brazil*

Brown Basilisk

Basiliscus vittatus

Characteristics: TL 30 inches (75 cm), SVL 10½ inches (26 cm). Males have head crest and flat dorsal crest.

Terrarium: Rainforest terrarium with large water container and vertically and horizontally arranged climbing branches the thickness of an arm. Moisture-retaining substrate 2–4 inches (5–10 cm) deep, kept slightly damp. Recommended terrarium size for housing an adult pair: 72 × 40 × 80 inches (180 × 100 × 200 cm). Air temperature 77–86°F (25–30°C), at night 68–71.5°F (20–22°C), water temperature 77°F (25°C), basking islands 104°F (40°C). Atmospheric humidity 70–90%. Lighting: 12–14 hours. UV radiation required.

Keeping/Care: Keep as a pair or in a group with one male. The larger and taller these shy, fidgety animals' terrarium, the less pronounced is their flight behavior, which quite often can result in injuries.

Diet: Field crickets, grasshoppers, wax moths, *Zophobas* larvae, freshwater fish, and young mice. Mineral supplements on a regular basis.

Behavior: In the wild, they are found near bodies of water; in the terrarium they enjoy swimming.

Terrarium type: 🌿
Level of difficulty: 2
Activity: ☀
Habit: 🌳

IN BRIEF **Class:** *Reptiles* **Order:** *Scaled reptiles* **Suborder:** *Lizards* **Family:** *Iguanas* **Range:** *Southern Mexico to Colombia*

Brown Water Snake

Nerodia taxispilota

Characteristics: TL 56 inches (140 cm), rarely up to 66 inches (175 cm). Males stay smaller. To ascertain sex, see page 15.

Terrarium type: 🔲
Level of difficulty: 2
Activity: ☀
Habit: 〰 ⬡

Terrarium: Woodland terrarium with 50% water portion. On the land portion, provide hiding places and retreats, as well as branches for climbing. Recommended terrarium size for housing an adult pair 56 inches (140 cm) long: 72 × 28 × 28 inches (180 × 70 × 70 cm). For each additional specimen, increase area by 20%. Air temperature 68–79°F (20–26°C), at night 59–70°F (15–21°C), water temperature 71.5–75°F (22–24°C), basking islands 86°F (30°C). Atmospheric humidity 60%. Lighting: 12 hours, partly UV.

Keeping/Care: Keep singly or as a group. Separate animals at feeding time. Hibernation: 8–12 weeks at 50–59°F (10–15°C). Requires frequent cleaning owing to its copious, watery, foul-smelling excrement.

Diet: Fish and pieces of fish, and young mammals and frogs.

Behavior: Lives near quiet bodies of water with overhanging branches. Very good swimmer and diver. Some individuals are quick to bite.

IN BRIEF **Class:** *Reptiles* **Order:** *Scaled reptiles*
Suborder: *Snakes* **Family:** *Colubrids* **Range:** *Southeastern United States*

Bullsnake

Pituophis melanoleucus sayi

Terrarium type: 🔼🔼
Level of difficulty: 2
Activity: ☼
Habit: ⤋⤋

Characteristics: TL up to 100 inches (250 cm). Adult females are longer. To ascertain sex, see page 15.

Terrarium: Semidry terrarium with climbing branches, large water dish, and hiding places under roots, flat stones, and pieces of cork. Substrate: mixture of loam, sand, soil, and leaves, 4–6 inches (10–15 cm) deep. Recommended terrarium size for 1–2 adults: 150 × 50 × 80 inches (250 × 125 × 200 cm). Air temperature 77–82.5°F (25–28°C), at night 64.5–68°F (18–20°C), basking islands up to 91.5°F (33°C). Atmospheric humidity in the daytime 50%, at night 60%. Lighting: 12 hours, partly UV.

Keeping/Care: These snakes are best kept singly because of their size. Specimens of northern origin should hibernate for 8–16 weeks at 48.5–50°F (6–10°C).

Diet: Mice, rats, hamsters, guinea pigs, chicks, and eggs.

Behavior: Largely diurnal. Mainly a ground-dwelling species, but occasionally climbs. Freshly captured specimens exhibit pronounced defensive behavior includes vibrating the tip of its tail, hissing, and pretending to bite, but most quickly become tame.

IN BRIEF **Class:** *Reptiles* **Order:** *Scaled reptiles* **Suborder:** *Snakes* **Family:** *Colubrids* **Range:** *Prairies and deserts; southern Canada to northern Mexico*

Burmese Python

Python molurus bivittatus

Characteristics: TL 240 inches (600 cm), occasionally up to 320 inches (800 cm). To ascertain sex, see page 15.

Terrarium type:
Level of difficulty: 2
Activity:
Habit:

Terrarium: Woodland terrarium with strong branches for climbing, large water basin, and hiding places on the ground. Recommended terrarium size for housing a pair up to 100 inches (250 cm) long: 100 × 48 × 72 inches (250 × 120 × 180 cm). Larger specimens need terrariums of up to 180 × 120 × 80 inches (450 × 300 × 200 cm). Air temperature 81–86°F (27–30°C), at night 71.5–77°F (22–25°C), water temperature 75–79°F (24–26°C), basking islands 95–104°F (35–40°C). Atmospheric humidity 60–70%, at night 80–90%. Lighting: 10–14 hours.

Keeping/Care: Though these pythons get along well with each other, keeping a group is not advisable because of their size. Do not overfeed to induce rapid growth as this leads to obesity.

Diet: Depending on size, rats, guinea pigs, rabbits, chicks, doves, chickens, and ducks.

Behavior: Good climber and swimmer. Not aggressive, but must always be handled with care because of its size.

IN BRIEF **Class:** *Reptiles* **Order:** *Scaled reptiles*
Suborder: *Snakes* **Family:** *Boas and pythons*
Range: *Indochina, southern China to Indonesia*

California King Snake

Lampropeltis getula californiae

Characteristics: TL 60 inches (150 cm), rarely 80 inches (200 cm). Ringed and striped forms known to exist. To ascertain sex, see page 15.

Terrarium type:
Level of difficulty: 1
Activity:
Habit:

Terrarium: Dry woodland terrarium with a climbing branch, hiding places on the ground, and a large water dish. Recommended terrarium size for housing an adult pair up to 60 inches (150 cm) long: 60 × 30 × 30 inches (150 × 75 × 75 cm). Air temperature 73.5–81°F (23–27°C), at night 59–68°F (15–20°C). Water temperature 64.5–68°F (18–20°C), basking islands 95°F (35°C). Atmospheric humidity 60–80%. Lighting: 12 hours, partly UV.

Keeping/Care: Keep singly, or keep only animals of the same size together. Always feed separately because of cannibalism. Hibernation: 3 months at 50–59°F (10–15°C).

Diet: Mice, rats, chicks, fish, and eggs.

Behavior: Sociable where their keepers are concerned. The species lives in deciduous and coniferous forests, but also in deserts.

IN BRIEF **Class:** *Reptiles* **Order:** *Scaled reptiles*
Suborder: *Snakes* **Family:** *Colubrids* **Range:** *Western United States, Oregon south to southern Baja peninsula*
Important: *Protected in California; virtually all specimens available as captive-raised.*

Cane Toad

Bufo marinus

Characteristics: Maximum SVL 10 inches (25 cm), but usually smaller. Weight up to 2.2 pounds (1 kg). Males stay much smaller and slimmer than females.

Terrarium type: ▭ ◮

Level of difficulty: 1 !

Activity: ▭ ☽

Habit: ▭

Terrarium: Rainforest terrarium with large water dish for soaking. Water level 2 inches (5 cm). Substrate 4 inches (10 cm) deep: woodland soil or peat-sand mixture, covered with moss. Provide hiding places. Recommended terrarium size for up to 3 adult specimens: about 80 × 40 × 24 inches (200 × 100 × 60 cm). Temperature 73.5–82.5°F (23–28°C), at night 68°F (20°C), water temperature 77°F (25°C). Atmospheric humidity 60% or greater. Lighting: 10–12 hours.

Keeping/Care: Keep only specimens of the same size (cannibalism).

Diet: Large insects, earthworms, frogs, lizards, snails, pinkie mice, and rats.

Behavior: The males' mating call is a high-pitched "brrrrr" sound.

IN BRIEF **Class:** *Amphibians* **Order:** *Frogs and toads*
Suborder: *Modern or advanced frogs* **Family:** *True toads*
Range: *Rainforests of Central and South America, introduced in parts of North America, Australia, and Southeast Asia*
Important: *These animals' skin secretions are poisonous; wash hands thoroughly after handling. If threatened, they can spray their toxin to a distance of 3.3 feet (1 m). Watch your eyes!*

Chacoan Horned Frog

Ceratophrys cranwelli

Also: Cranwell's horned frog

Characteristics: SVL up to 5³⁄₁₆ inches (13 cm). Males stay smaller, with loose, dark-spotted throats.

Terrarium type: 〰
Level of difficulty: 1 !
Activity: ☼
Habit: 🌱

Terrarium: Wet terrarium with soil substrate about 4 inches (10 cm) deep; keep slightly moist. Provide places to hide under cork bark, flat stones, and roots. This frog burrows often, so it is best to keep plants in flower pots. Supply a large water dish. Recommended terrarium size for housing one adult specimen: 48 × 24 × 24 inches (120 × 60 × 60 cm). Air temperature 75–82.5°F (24–28°C), at night 68–71.5°F (20–22°C). Atmospheric humidity 80%. Lighting: 10–12 hours.

Keeping/Care: Keep singly because of aggressive behavior and cannibalism. Keep terrarium well ventilated to prevent standing water. These animals produce large quantities of feces, so you need to change the substrate frequently.

Diet: House crickets, field crickets, cockroaches, grasshoppers, earthworms, baby mammals. Supply mineral/vitamin supplement.

Behavior: Likes to burrow into the substrate. These frogs have teeth and bite quite readily. Use caution when you put your hand into the terrarium.

IN BRIEF **Class:** *Amphibians* **Order:** *Frogs and toads* **Suborder:** *Modern or advanced frogs* **Family:** *Neotropical or neodactylid frogs* **Range:** *Brazil, Argentina, Bolivia, and Paraguay*

Chilean Dwarf Tegu

Callopistes maculatus

Characteristics: TL up to 20 inches (50 cm), SVL 8¾ inches (22 cm). Males larger and heavier, with larger femoral pores (see page 26) and reddish belly.

Terrarium type: 🌵
Level of difficulty: 1
Activity: ☀
Habit: 🔺

Terrarium: Steppe terrarium. Supply places to bask and hide, layer flat stone slabs to form a cave. Place them so that the slabs can't be undermined or made to collapse, however. Substrate: layer of gravel or sand with loam, about 4–6 inches (10–15 cm) deep. Plant with robust plants in flower pots. Recommended terrarium size for housing an adult pair: 72 × 40 × 24 inches (180 × 100 × 60 cm). Temperature 77–95°F (25–35°C), at night 64.5–71.5°F (18–22°C), basking islands 104°F (40°C). Atmospheric humidity 40–60%. Lighting: 12–14 hours. UV radiation required.

Keeping/Care: Keep as a pair or as a group with one male. Hibernation: If desired, 8–12 weeks at 50–59°F (10–15°C).

Diet: House crickets, field crickets, wax moth larvae, and baby mammals. Some will accept sweet fruits or eggs. Mineral supplements regularly.

Behavior: Quite shy. Likes to dig.

IN BRIEF **Class:** *Reptiles* **Order:** *Scaled reptiles* **Suborder:** *Lizards* **Family:** *Whiptail lizards and their allies (tegus)* **Range:** *Northern to central Chile*

Chilean Rose Tarantula

Grammostola spatulata

Terrarium type: 🏔🏔
Level of difficulty: 1 !
Activity: ☼ ☽
Habit: ↟

Characteristics: Body up to 2½ inches (6 cm) long. See page 9 for sexing. The front part of the adult male's body is a brighter metallic pink.

Terrarium: Woodland terrarium. Loam and sand substrate, 4–6 inches (10–15 cm) deep, kept only slightly damp. Provide a flat stone or flat piece of wood under which the spider can dig its hole. Supply a shallow water dish. Recommended terrarium size for one adult: 12 × 12 × 5 inches (30 × 30 × 20 cm). Temperature 68–71.5°F (20–22°C), in places 77°F (25°C), at night 61–68°F (16–20°C). Atmospheric humidity 60–80%. Lighting: 8–10 hours.

Keeping/Care: Keep male or female singly. Place together only to attempt mating.

Diet: Depending on size, flies, house crickets, grasshoppers, cockroaches, and baby mammals.

Behavior: Peaceful species. Digs shallow holes to live in. Be careful when working on the terrarium because of the species' defensive behavior when disturbed. Watch out for the urticating hairs! Its bite is not considered dangerous to humans.

Similar needs: *Grammostola cala, Grammostola rosea*

IN BRIEF **Class:** *Arachnids* **Order:** *Spiders*
Suborder: *Tarantulas and relatives* **Family:** *Tarantulas*
Range: *Chile, Bolivia, and Argentina*

Chinese Fire-bellied Newt

Cynops orientalis

Also: Chinese dwarf newt

Characteristics: TL up to 3⅝ inches (9 cm), SVL 1⅝ inches (4 cm). Males smaller and thinner. During mating season, males are recognizable by the swollen cloaca (see page 26).

Terrarium type: 〰

Level of difficulty: 1

Activity: ☼

Habit: ⩫ �

Terrarium: Aquatic terrarium with predominating water portion and slight incline leading to land portion. Tank size of 32 × 14 × 16 inches (80 × 35 × 40 cm) is adequate for 6–8 adult specimens. Furnish with roots and stones as hiding places and dry places to sit. Water temperature 59–68°F (15–20°C), in summer also to 71.5°F (22°C). Subdued lighting for 10–12 hours.

Keeping/Care: Keep as a pair or a group. The aquatic terrarium must not be left open at the top, as these newts are excellent climbers even on smooth surfaces.

Diet: Mosquito larvae, water fleas, *Tubifex*, earthworms, and slugs. It's best to feed them in the water, where live food can't escape.

Behavior: In the wild, lives in quiet bodies of water.

IN BRIEF   **Class:** *Amphibians* **Order:** *Salamanders*
Suborder: *Salamanders and their allies* **Family:** *Salamanders and newts* **Range:** *Central to southeastern China*

Chinese Water Dragon

Physignathus cocincinus

Terrarium type: ⌒

Level of difficulty: 2

Activity: ☼

Habit: 🌳

Characteristics: TL 37–40 inches (80–100 cm), SVL 8–10 inches (20–25 cm). Males bigger overall, with larger crest and larger femoral pores (see page 26).

Terrarium: Aquatic terrarium with 50% water portion and water level of 8–10 inches (20–25 cm). Change water regularly. Provide sturdy branches for climbing. Recommended terrarium size for housing an adult pair 40 inches (100 cm) long: 80 × 40 × 40 inches (200 × 100 × 100 cm). Add 15% for each additional female. Air temperature 77–86°F (25–30°C), at night 68–77°F (20–25°C), water temperature 77°F (25°C), basking islands 113°F (45°C). Atmospheric humidity 80–90%. Lighting: 12–14 hours. UV radiation required.

Keeping/Care: Keep as a pair or as a group with only one male. These agamas easily injure themselves by impetuous flight behavior.

Diet: Insects, giant mealworms, fish, small mammals, fruits, and mineral supplements.

Behavior: When threatened, this species dives into the water.

Similar needs: Eastern water dragon (*Physignathus lesueurii*)

IN BRIEF **Class:** *Reptiles* **Order:** *Scaled reptiles* **Suborder:** *Lizards* **Family:** *Agamas* **Range:** *Myanmar, Laos, Cambodia, Vietnam, Thailand to southern China*

Chuckwalla

Sauromalus obesus

Characteristics: TL 14–16 inches (35–40 cm), SVL 7⅛–8 inches (18–20 cm). Males have bigger body, wider head, thicker, shorter tail, and prominent femoral pores (see page 26).

Terrarium type:	🌵
Level of difficulty:	2
Activity:	☀
Habit:	◺

Terrarium: Dry terrarium with stable pile of stones under which the animals can climb, bask, and hide. Small water bowl. Substrate of sand and gravel, about 2–4 inches (5–10 cm) deep, suitable for digging. Recommended terrarium size for housing an adult pair: 48 × 32 × 24 inches (120 × 80 × 60 cm). Temperature 86–100°F (30–38°C), at night 64.5–68°F (18–20°C), basking islands 104°F (40°C). Mist weekly in the morning. Lighting: 14 hours. UV radiation required.

Keeping/Care: Keep as a pair or as a group with one male. Hibernation: 10–12 weeks at 64.5–68°F (18–20°C). Young specimens adapt better to captivity than adults.

Diet: Leafy plants and herbs, including romaine lettuce and dandelions. Vegetables such as chopped carrots and celery. Fruits such as grapes, bananas, and berries. Some accept worms and grasshoppers. Mineral supplements.

Behavior: Avoids open sandy areas. If frightened, they hide.

IN BRIEF **Class:** *Reptiles* **Order:** *Scaled reptiles* **Suborder:** *Lizards* **Family:** *Iguanas* **Range:** *Southwestern United States to Mexico*

Cobalt Blue Tarantula

Haplopelma lividum

Also: *Melopoeus lividum*

Characteristics: Body up to 2½ inches (6 cm). See page 9 for sex determination.

Terrarium type: 🗠

Level of difficulty: 3 !

Activity: 🌄 🌙

Habit: 🔽

Terrarium: Woodland terrarium with substrate of slightly damp humus, 4–6 inches (10–15 cm) deep. Caves of cork bark with a diameter of about 6 inches (15 cm). Supply shallow water dish. Recommended terrarium size for one adult specimen: 16 × 12 × 12 inches (40 × 30 × 30 cm). Temperature 75–82.5°F (24–28°C), at night 68–71.5°F (20–22°C). Atmospheric humidity up to 85%. Lighting: 8–10 hours.

Keeping/Care: Keep these spiders singly. Shy, but extremely defensive; does not possess urticating hairs.

Diet: Depending on size, flies, wax moths, house crickets, field crickets, grasshoppers, cockroaches, baby rodents.

Behavior: Prefers to stay in the cave where it lives. Quickly attacks everything that moves. Be extremely careful when you're doing work in the terrarium.

IN BRIEF **Class:** *Arachnids* **Order:** *Spiders*
Suborder: *Tarantulas and relatives* **Family:** *Tarantulas*
Range: *Southeastern India, Burma, Thailand, Singapore, and Malaysia*

Collared Lizard

Crotaphytus collaris

Also: Eastern collared lizard

Characteristics: Depending on sub-species, TL up to 14⅛ inches (36 cm), SVL 4¾ inches (12 cm). Males more brilliantly colored, with wider head and tail thickened at the base.

Terrarium type: 🌵
Level of difficulty: 2
Activity: ☀
Habit:

Terrarium: Steppe terrarium with stable pile of stones and large roots as hiding places. Cover rear and side walls. Substrate at least 4 inches (10 cm) deep, suitable for digging. Include artificial or drought-tolerant plants in flower pots. Provide small water container. Recommended terrarium size for housing an adult pair: 60 × 24 × 32 inches (150 × 60 × 80 cm). Temperature 82.5–95°F (28–35°C), at night 64.5–71.5°F (18–22°C), basking islands 113°F (45°C). Atmospheric humidity 40–60%. Lighting: 14 hours. UV radiation required.

Keeping/Care: Keep as a pair or as a group with only one male. Direct heat lamp onto a flat stone or provide heat rock. Hibernation: 8–12 weeks at 50–59°F (10–15°C).

Diet: Field crickets, grasshoppers, cockroaches, other lizards, and baby mammals. Occasionally flowers, leaves, fruit.

Behavior: Very active species, likes to bask. Cannibalistic. Do not keep with smaller lizards.

IN BRIEF **Class:** *Reptiles* **Order:** *Scaled reptiles*
Suborder: *Lizards* **Family:** *Iguanas* **Range:** *Southern United States to northwestern Mexico*

Colombian Rainbow Boa

Epicrates cenchria maurus

Characteristics: TL up to 80 inches (200 cm). Males stay somewhat smaller. To ascertain sex, see page 15.

Terrarium: Rainforest terrarium with a firmly anchored branch for climbing and places to hide on the ground. Substrate: 2 inches (5 cm) deep, mixture of sand and soil; keep moderately damp, but dry above the under-tank heat source. Set up a large water container. Recommended terrarium size for housing an adult pair: 80 × 40 × 60 inches (200 × 100 × 150 cm). For each additional specimen, increase area by 20%. Air temperature 81–86°F (27–30°C), at night 73.5–79°F (23–26°C), water temperature 77°F (25°C), basking islands 95°F (35°C). Atmospheric humidity 60–70%, at night 80–90%. Lighting: 10–12 hours.

Keeping/Care: Keep as a pair or in groups with one male. Make sure ventilation is good. Wild-caught specimens can be very defensive and reluctant to feed.

Diet: Mice, rats, and day-old chicks.

Behavior: Good climber and swimmer.

Terrarium type:
Level of difficulty: 1
Activity:
Habit:

IN BRIEF **Class:** *Reptiles* **Order:** *Scaled reptiles* **Suborder:** *Snakes* **Family:** *Boas and pythons* **Range:** *Costa Rica, northern Colombia, Venezuela and offshore islands*

Common Egg-Eater

Dasypeltis scabra

Also: African egg-eater, rhombic egg-eater

Terrarium type: 🐾
Level of difficulty: 2
Activity: ☀ 🌙
Habit: 🌳

Characteristics: TL 28 inches (70 cm), rarely up to 44 inches (110 cm). Females are larger and can be identified by their smaller number of abdominal scales.

Terrarium: Semidry terrarium with several branches for climbing. Hiding places under stones and cork slabs and in cork tubes. Supply a water pan for bathing. Recommended terrarium size for housing an adult pair 28 inches (70 cm) long: 32 × 16 × 32 inches (80 × 40 × 80 cm). To keep a third, add 20% to the area. Air temperature 71.5–82.5°F (22–28°C), at night 64.5–71.5°F (18–22°C), basking islands 86°F (30°C). Atmospheric humidity 50–60%. Lighting: 10–12 hours, partly UV.

Keeping/Care: Very compatible with one another. In winter, keep 7°F (4°C) cooler in the daytime and at night. Lighting: 6 hours.

Diet: Nothing but eggs; depending on size, finch, parakeet, quail, or hen eggs. Shells are regurgitated.

Behavior: Arboreal, but often seen on the ground as well. If making a defensive display, it rubs its scales together to make a noise, inflates its throat, hisses, and bites in imitation of a venomous snake.

IN BRIEF Class: *Reptiles* **Order:** *Scaled reptiles*
Suborder: *Snakes* **Family:** *Colubrids* **Range:** *Northeastern to southern Africa, southern Arabia*

Common House Gecko

Hemidactylus frenatus

Also: Asian house gecko, chichak, spiny-tailed house gecko

Characteristics: TL 5⅝ inches (14 cm), SVL up to 2¹³⁄₁₆ inches (7 cm). Males more massive, with bigger heads and larger preanal pores (see page 27).

Terrarium type: 🌿
Level of difficulty: 1
Activity: ☽
Habit: 🌳

Terrarium: Woodland terrarium; keep substrate moist. The species is tolerant regarding its environment and will thrive equally well in a dry terrarium. Provide places for climbing and hiding. Recommended terrarium size for housing an adult pair: 16 × 16 × 24 inches (40 × 40 × 60 cm). Add 15% more area for each additional female. Temperature 77–86°F (25–30°C), at night 68–71.5°F (20–22°C). Atmospheric humidity 70–80%. Lighting: 10–12 hours.

Keeping/Care: The species is popular because these animals need only relatively small terrariums. Keep as a pair or as a group with only one male.

Diet: House crickets, moths, or spiders.

Behavior: Very good climber. Called "chichak" because of its chirping and screeching vocalizations. Lives throughout Asia near rocks, palms, and houses.

IN BRIEF **Class:** *Reptiles* **Order:** *Scaled reptiles* **Suborder:** *Lizards* **Family:** *Geckos* **Range:** *Entire Asian area, introduced into Mexico to Panama*

Common Musk Turtle

Sternotherus odoratus

Also: *Kinosternum odoratum*

Characteristics: CL up to 5⅜ inches (14 cm). Males have longer tails, with a blunt horny nail at the end.

Terrarium type: ⌇
Level of difficulty: 1
Activity: ☼
Habit: ◌

Terrarium: Aquatic terrarium with ¾ water portion. Water level: 5³⁄₁₆ inches (13 cm). Clean water regularly. Provide visual barriers and places to hide above and below water. Recommended minimum area (length × width) of a terrarium for housing an adult pair: 32 × 14 inches (80 × 35 cm). Air temperature 73.5–81°F (23–27°C), at night 64.5–71.5°F (18–22°C), water temperature 68–77°F (20–25°C), basking islands 95–104°F (35–40°C). Lighting: up to 12 hours. UV radiation required.

Diet: Earthworms, insects, snails, and pieces of fish. Gelatin-based foods and dry foods for aquatic turtles.

Behavior: Seldom leaves the water portion. When threatened, exudes a foul-smelling secretion from its musk glands (hence the name!).

IN BRIEF **Class:** *Reptiles* **Order:** *Tortoises and turtles*
Suborder: *Common-necked or straight-necked turtles*
Family: *Mud and musk turtles* **Range:** *Southern Canada to northern Mexico*

Common Reed Frog

Hyperolius viridiflavus

Characteristics: SVL up to 1⅝ inches (4 cm). Males stay smaller, are unobtrusively colored, have dark throat and large vocal sac.

Terrarium type:	🌿 〰️
Level of difficulty:	2
Activity:	☀️ 🌙
Habit:	↟↟ 💧

Terrarium: Rainforest terrarium with large water dish. Alternatively, aquatic terrarium with ¾ water portion; water level 2–4 inches (5–10 cm). Transition to land portion can be created with peat slabs. Moisture-retaining substrate 2⅞–5⅛ inches (7–13 cm) deep, can be covered with moss in parts. Provide branches for climbing. Plant green and climbing plants. Recommended terrarium size for up to 6 adults: 24 × 16 × 24 inches (60 × 40 × 60 cm). Air temperature 77–82.5°F (25–28°C), in places 86°F (30°C), at night 64.5–71.5°F (18–22°C). Atmospheric humidity at least 50%. Lighting: 12–14 hours.

Keeping/Care: Males compete for calling places, but do not engage in serious fighting. As a breeding group, keep 2 males with 4 females.

Diet: Flies, wax moths, small house crickets, and field crickets.

Behavior: Once habituated to the terrarium, common reed frogs sometimes hunt for food in the daytime as well.

IN BRIEF **Class:** *Amphibians* **Order:** *Frogs and toads* **Suborder:** *Modern or advanced frogs* **Family:** *African tree frogs* **Range:** *Central to southern Africa*

Corn Snake

Pantherophis guttatus guttatus

Also: *Elaphe guttata guttata*

Characteristics: TL about 48 inches (120 cm), in some cases even up to 72 inches (180 cm).

Terrarium type:
Level of difficulty: 1
Activity:
Habit:

Terrarium: Woodland terrarium with a bathing pan that can accommodate the snake. Provide climbing branches and hiding places. Recommended terrarium size for housing an adult pair up to 48 inches (120 cm) long: 48 × 24 × 48 inches (120 × 60 × 120 cm). To keep a third specimen, add 20% to area. Air temperature 71.5–82.5°F (22–28°C), at night 64.5–68°F (18–20°C), water temperature 64.5–71.5°F (18–22°C), basking islands 82.5–90°F (28–32°C). Atmospheric humidity 50–70%. Lighting: 12 hours, partly UV. Spotlight for basking recommended.

Keeping/Care: Keeping several specimens is easy, provided they are the same size. Hibernation: November to February at 53.5–59°F (12–15°C), with decreased activity and without feeding, but not essential.

Diet: Mice or rats of appropriate size. Easily adapts to eating prekilled feeder animals.

Behavior: Primarily diurnal, but in some cases also crepuscular and nocturnal. Likes to climb. Many color mutations available.

IN BRIEF **Class:** *Reptiles* **Order:** *Scaled reptiles* **Suborder:** *Snakes* **Family:** *Colubrids* **Range:** *Central and eastern United States to northern Mexico*

Costa Rican Tiger-rump Tarantula

Cyclosternum fasciata

Also: *Cyclosternum fasciatus, Cyclosternum fasciatum*

Characteristics: Body up to 1⅝ inches (4 cm). Sexually mature males identifiable by tibial spurs.

Terrarium type: 🌿
Level of difficulty: 2 !
Activity: 🌅 🌙
Habit: ↡↡

Terrarium: Rainforest terrarium. Substrate of loose leaf mold, about 1¼–2 inches (3–5 cm) deep, suitable for digging; can be covered with leaves. Include roots or pieces of wood under which the spider can make its holes. Supply water container. Recommended terrarium size for one adult: 12 × 8 × 12 inches (30 × 20 × 30 cm). Temperature 73.5–79°F (23–26°C), at night 64.5–68°F (18–20°C). Atmospheric humidity 70–80%. Lighting: 8–10 hours.

Keeping/Care: Keep male or female singly. Be careful when working on the terrarium, as this generally shy species is quite nervous and quick to defend itself by flicking hairs (see page 20).

Diet: Depending on size, flies, small house crickets, field crickets, and grasshoppers.

Behavior: Hole-digging, hair-flicking spider. Behavior is nervous to defensive, but not too prone to bite.

Similar needs: *Metriopelma zebrata*

IN BRIEF **Class:** *Arachnids* **Order:** *Spiders*
Suborder: *Tarantulas and relatives* **Family:** *Tarantulas*
Range: *Rainforests, Guatemala to Costa Rica*

Costa Rican Zebra Tarantula

Aphonopelma seemanni

Also: *Stripe knee tarantula*

Characteristics: Depending on subspecies, body 2½–3¼ inches (6–8 cm). After the final molt, the males lose the striped pattern typical of the species and are dark brown to black in color.

Terrarium type: [icon]
Level of difficulty: 1!
Activity: [icon] [icon]
Habit: [icon]

Terrarium: Woodland or grassland terrarium with soil substrate mixture 2–4 inches (5–10 cm) deep. Provide caves made of cork bark with diameter of about 6 inches (15 cm). Supply shallow water dish. Recommended terrarium size for housing one adult: 16 × 12 × 12 inches (40 × 30 × 30 cm). Temperature 75–82.5°F (24–28°C), at night 68–73.5°F (20–23°C). Atmospheric humidity 60–80%. Lighting: 8–10 hours.

Keeping/Care: Keep male or female singly. Be careful when working on the terrarium; the species is nervous and easily stressed.

Diet: Depending on size, flies, house crickets, grasshoppers, and baby mammals.

Behavior: Builds tube-like hiding places in which it stays most of the time. An easily maintained and attractive species for the beginner, but do not attempt to handle.

IN BRIEF **Class:** *Arachnids* **Order:** *Spiders*
Suborder: *Tarantulas and relatives* **Family:** *Tarantulas*
Range: *California, Texas, Mexico to Costa Rica*

Crevice Spiny Lizard

Sceloporus poinsettii

Terrarium type: 🌵
Level of difficulty: 1
Activity: ☼
Habit:

Characteristics: TL up to 10 inches (25 cm), SVL 4⅜ inches (11 cm). Males have turquoise-blue throat, bright blue and black stripes on the sides of the belly, and prominent femoral pores (see page 26).

Terrarium: Desert terrarium with piles of stones and rocks that provide hiding places. Substrate: sand or gravel, 2½–3¼ inches (5–8 cm) deep, kept slightly damp near the roots of heat-tolerant plants such as succulents. Recommended terrarium size for housing an adult pair: 40 × 20 × 24 inches (100 × 50 × 60 cm). Temperature 77–86°F (25–30°C), at night 61–68°F (16–20°C), basking islands 104°F (40°C). Atmospheric humidity 50–70%. Lighting: 14 hours. UV radiation required.

Keeping/Care: Keep as a pair or as a group with one male; in larger terrariums, also can be kept with several males. Hibernation: 12 weeks at 59–68°F (15–20°C) if breeding is desired.

Diet: House crickets, cockroaches, field crickets, grasshoppers, wax moths and their larvae, and baby mammals. Occasionally, leaves and flowers.

Behavior: Ground and rock dweller. Live-bearing.

IN BRIEF **Class:** *Reptiles* **Order:** *Scaled reptiles* **Suborder:** *Lizards* **Family:** *Iguanas* **Range:** *Southern United States to Mexico*

Cuban Brown Anole

Anolis sagrei

Also: Caribbean anole, brown anole
Characteristics: TL 8 inches (20 cm), SVL 2½–2⅞ inches (6–7 cm). Females ⅓ smaller, with diamond-shaped spot pattern. Males have vertical pattern, fading to a uniform brown in adult specimens.

Terrarium type:
Level of difficulty: 1
Activity:
Habit:

Terrarium: Humid woodland terrarium with many places to climb. Substrate: sand-soil mixture; cover with leaves. Provide hiding places under pieces of bark and dense plantings. Recommended terrarium size for housing an adult pair: 32 × 24 × 24 inches (80 × 60 × 60 cm). Temperature 77–86°F (25–30°C), at night 63–71.5°F (17–22°C), basking islands 104°F (40°C). Atmospheric humidity 60–70%, at night 80–90%. Lighting: 12–14 hours. UV radiation required.

Keeping/Care: Keep as a pair or as a group with only one male. Hibernation: 8 weeks at 68–75°F (20–24°C).

Diet: House crickets, field crickets, grasshoppers, and beetles.

Behavior: Lives in open country, underbrush, near walls and fences. Climbs only short distances.

IN BRIEF **Class:** *Reptiles* **Order:** *Scaled reptiles*
Suborder: *Lizards* **Family:** *Iguanas* **Range:** *Caribbean islands, Atlantic coast from Florida to Mexico and Guatemala to Belize*

Curly-haired Tarantula

Brachypelma albopilosum

Characteristics: Body up to 3¼ inches (8 cm). Adult males with bulbous pedipalps.

Terrarium type: 🔼🔼
Level of difficulty: 1
Activity: 🔆)
Habit: 🔽

Terrarium: Moist woodland terrarium. Soil substrate about 2 inches (5 cm) deep; must be kept slightly damp. Crumbled moss or sphagnum peat moss can also be mixed into the substrate. Provide caves under stones or made of cork bark, with a diameter of about 6 inches (15 cm). Supply a shallow water dish. Recommended terrarium size for one adult: 16 × 12 × 12 inches (40 × 30 × 30 cm). Temperature 77–81°F (25–27°C), at night 64.5–68°F (18–20°C). Atmospheric humidity 70–80%. Lighting: 8–10 hours.

Keeping/Care: Keep a male or a female singly.

Diet: Depending on size, flies, house crickets, grasshoppers, and baby mammals.

Behavior: Peaceful creature. This species lives in caves dug in the substrate. It is less quick than other species to feel threatened when you are working on the terrarium. Only rarely does it flick hairs in self-defense (see page 20). A good beginner's tarantula.

IN BRIEF **Class:** *Arachnids* **Order:** *Spiders*
Suborder: *Tarantulas and relatives* **Family:** *Tarantulas*
Range: *Guatemala to Costa Rica*

Curly-tailed Lizard

Leiocephalus personatus

Terrarium type: 🌵
Level of difficulty: 1
Activity: ☀
Habit: 〰 ⬠

Characteristics: TL 10 inches (25 cm), SVL to 4 inches (10 cm). Males display two enlarged postanal scales (see page 27). Smaller and more plainly colored males greatly resemble the females, and unfortunately are often mistaken for them.

Terrarium: Dry terrarium with hiding and climbing places, sandy runs, and basking places. Recommended terrarium size for housing an adult pair: 48 × 24 × 24 inches (120 × 60 × 60 cm). Temperature 77–86°F (25–30°C), at night 64.5–68°F (18–20°C), basking islands 95–104°F (35–40°C). Atmospheric humidity 60%, at night 70–80%. Lighting: 12 hours. UV radiation required.

Keeping/Care: Keep only as a single animal or pair. Males and females are very territorial. Hibernation: 2 months at 68–71.5°F (20–22°C) during the day, 61–64.5°F (16–18°C) at night.

Diet: Insects such as house crickets, field crickets, flies, darkling beetle larvae, cockroaches, and small grasshoppers. Some individuals accept fruit and flowers.

Behavior: In the wild, found in savannah forests to brush-covered rocky countryside with adequate vegetation.

IN BRIEF **Class:** *Reptiles* **Order:** *Scaled reptiles* **Suborder:** *Lizards* **Family:** *Iguanas* **Range:** *Haiti and Dominican Republic*

Death Stalker

Leiurus quinquestriatus

Characteristics: TL up to 5¼ inches (13 cm). Males have distinctly larger teeth or pectines than females.

Terrarium type: 🌵
Level of difficulty: 3 !
Activity: ☽
Habit: 〰

Terrarium: Desert terrarium with substrate that is a mix of sand and loamy soil, barely 4 inches (10 cm) deep, suitable for digging. Supply shallow water dish. Recommended terrarium size for one adult: 12 × 12 × 8 inches (30 × 30 × 20 cm). Temperature 86–95°F (30–35°C), at night 68–77°F (20–25°C). Atmospheric humidity 40–50%. Lighting: 8–10 hours.

Keeping/Care: Keep males and females singly except for attemped breeding because of the pronounced interspecies aggressiveness. A very dangerous and potentially deadly species. Not for beginners. Secure terrarium tightly to prevent escape.

Diet: House crickets, field crickets, grasshoppers, cockroaches, mealworms, beetles, and *Zophobas* larvae.

Behavior: They dig caves under flat stones and retreat to them during the day.

IN BRIEF **Class:** *Arachnids* **Order:** *Scorpions*
Suborder: *Neoscorpionina* **Family:** *Thick-tailed scorpions*
Range: *North Africa, Arabian peninsula, Middle East to Turkey*
Important: *Not only one of the most poisonous scorpions, but also the quickest to sting. Stings affect the central nervous system and cause serious heart and circulatory problems.*

Desert Horned Lizard

Phrynosoma platyrhinos

Terrarium type: 🌵
Level of difficulty: 3
Activity: ☀
Habit: 〰

Characteristics: TL 5⅛ inches (13 cm), SVL 2½–3¼ inches (6–8 cm). Females somewhat larger and more massive. Males have enlarged postanal scales (see page 27).

Terrarium: Dry terrarium with hiding places under stones and pieces of roots. Sand and gravel substrate, about 4–6 inches (10–15 cm) deep, kept slightly damp in one corner. Plant with succulents. Recommended terrarium size for housing an adult pair: 32 × 20 × 20 inches (80 × 50 × 50 cm). Temperature 86–104°F (30–40°C), at night 64.5–68°F (18–20°C), basking islands 113°F (45°C). Atmospheric humidity 40–60%. Lighting: 14 hours. UV radiation required.

Keeping/Care: Keep as a pair or as a group with one male. Hibernation: 4 months at 50–59°F (10–15°C), slowly lowering the temperature over the course of several days. Sensitive to wet and cold substrate.

Diet: Mainly large ants such as harvester and honeypot ants.

Behavior: Gets moisture through its food.

IN BRIEF **Class:** *Reptiles* **Order:** *Scaled reptiles* **Suborder:** *Lizards* **Family:** *Iguanas* **Range:** *Oregon, California, Arizona to Mexico* **Important:** *Because of their specialized diets, horned lizards generally do not thrive in captivity and are best avoided.*

Desert Iguana

Dipsosaurus dorsalis

Characteristics: TL up to 16⅛ inches (41 cm), SVL up to 6 inches (15 cm). Males somewhat bigger and identifiable by clearly visible "swellings" at the base of the tail.

Terrarium type:
Level of difficulty: 3
Activity:
Habit:

Terrarium: Desert terrarium with a substrate at least 8 inches (20 cm) deep, suitable for digging. Make sure decorations will not be toppled if undermined. Plants in pots are best. Provide hiding and climbing places. Recommended terrarium size for housing an adult pair: 60 × 24 × 24 inches (150 × 60 × 60 cm). Air temperature 86–104°F (30–40°C), at night 64.5–71.5°F (18–22°C), basking islands 113–122°F (45–50°C). Atmospheric humidity 30–40%. Lighting: 14 hours. UV radiation required.

Keeping/Care: Keep as a pair or in groups with one male. For 2 months in winter, reduce temperature to 68°F (20°C) and lighting to 6 hours at most.

Diet: Foods of plant origin; predominantly leafy plants such as romaine lettuce or dandelion greens. Vegetables such as summer squashes and fruit in addition. Dandelion and hibiscus flowers are gladly accepted. Animal food in very small amounts.

Behavior: Needs a great deal of warmth, but make wonderful pets.

IN BRIEF **Class:** *Reptiles* **Order:** *Scaled reptiles* **Suborder:** *Lizards* **Family:** *Iguanas* **Range:** *Southwestern United States to northwestern Mexico*

Desert Spiny Lizard

Sceloporus magister

Characteristics: TL up to 11³⁄₁₆ inches (28 cm), SVL 4¾ inches (12 cm). Males have enlarged postanal scales and femoral pores (see page 26). Females are slightly smaller.

Terrarium type: 🌵
Level of difficulty: 1
Activity: ☼
Habit: ▄▄ ◺

Terrarium: Desert terrarium with shallow water dish and sandy substrate about 4 inches (10 cm) deep. Provide climbing places and hiding places under piles of stones. Plant with robust, heat-tolerant species such as succulents. Keep substrate slightly damp near roots of plants. Recommended terrarium size for housing an adult pair: 40 × 24 × 24 inches (100 × 60 × 60 cm). Temperature 82.5–91.5°F (28–33°C), at night 68–71.5°F (20–22°C), basking islands 104–113°F (40–45°C). Atmospheric humidity 50–70%. Bright lighting: 14 hours. UV radiation required.

Keeping/Care: Keep as a pair or as a group with only one male. Hibernation: 4–6 weeks at 50–59°F (10–15°C), to promote reproduction.

Diet: House crickets, cockroaches, field crickets, grasshoppers, wax moths and their larvae, baby rodents. Now and then, flowers and fruits.

Behavior: Very adept at climbing.

IN BRIEF **Class:** *Reptiles* **Order:** *Scaled reptiles*
Suborder: *Lizards* **Family:** *Iguanas* **Range:** *Southwestern United States and northwestern Mexico*

Dragon Agama

Japalura splendida

Also: banana-split lizard, green-stripe dragon

Characteristics: TL 12 inches (30 cm), SVL 4¾ inches (12 cm). Sexes visually indistinguishable.

Terrarium type: 🔺🔺
Level of difficulty: 3
Activity: ☀
Habit: 🌳 ⬗

Terrarium: Woodland terrarium with lots of climbing branches and dense plantings that provide hiding places. Include container for bathing. Recommended terrarium size for housing an adult pair: 24 × 20 × 28 inches (60 × 50 × 70 cm). Mist terrarium 2–3 times weekly. Temperature 77–82.5°F (25–28°C), at night 61–68°F (16–20°C), basking islands 104°F (40°C). Atmospheric humidity 70–80%. Lighting: 12–14 hours. UV radiation required.

Keeping/Care: Good terrarium ventilation required. Keep as a pair or in a group with one male. Can be kept outdoors from May to September. Hibernation: 10–12 weeks at 43–46.5°F (6–8°C).

Diet: Field crickets, house crickets, grasshoppers, cockroaches, wax moths and their larvae, and mealworms plus vitamin/mineral supplementation.

Behavior: Turn brownish color under stress.

Caution: Some of the commercially available species might not be *Japalura splendida*, and require different living conditions from those described.

IN BRIEF **Class:** *Reptiles* **Order:** *Scaled reptiles* **Suborder:** *Lizards* **Family:** *Agamas* **Range:** *Western China*

Dull Day Gecko

Phelsuma dubia

Characteristics: TL 6 inches (15 cm), SVL 2¾ inches (7 cm). Adult males identifiable by stronger build, thicker head, and preanofemoral pores (see page 27).

Terrarium type: ⛲
Level of difficulty: 1
Activity: ☀
Habit: 🌳

Terrarium: Moist semiwet terrarium. Furnish with smooth-leaved plants such as *Sansevieria* and smooth climbing branches such as bamboo stalks. Provide hiding places. Recommended terrarium size for housing an adult pair: 16 × 16 × 24 inches (40 × 40 × 60 cm). Add 15% to area for each additional female. Temperature 77–84.5°F (24–29°C), at night 64.5–71.5°F (18–22°C). Atmospheric humidity 50–60%, at night 70–80%. Lighting: 10–12 hours. UV radiation required.

Keeping/Care: Keep as a pair or as a group with only one male. These geckos' beautiful colors are most effective in strong lighting.

Diet: Field crickets, house crickets, and wax moths or their larvae. Once a week, mashed fruit. Mineral supplementation important for formation of hard-shelled eggs.

Behavior: In the wild, found on banana species, coconut palms, but also on house walls.

IN BRIEF **Class:** *Reptiles* **Order:** *Scaled reptiles* **Suborder:** *Lizards* **Family:** *Geckos* **Range:** *Madagascar, Comoros, Zanzibar, and Tanzania*

Dyeing Poison Frog

Dendrobates tinctorius

Characteristics: SVL 1⅝ inches (4 cm), in some populations up to 2¾ inches (7 cm). Males have much larger, heart-shaped finger discs.

Terrarium type: 🌿
Level of difficulty: 2
Activity: ☼
Habit: ▄▄

Terrarium: Rainforest terrarium with 20% water portion or large water dish. Substrate: peat slabs or humus. Coconut shells as places to hide or lay eggs. Recommended terrarium size for housing an adult pair: 24 × 16 × 16 inches (60 × 40 × 40 cm). Increase area by 50% to house a group of up to 4 specimens. Temperature 73.5–82.5°F (23–28°C), at night 64.5–68°F (18–20°C). Atmospheric humidity 80%, at night up to 100%. Lighting: 12–14 hours.

Keeping/Care: Keep as a pair or as a group with one male and 2–3 females. Do not keep together with other ground-dwelling dendrobated species because crossbreeding may occur.

Diet: Small insects such as fruit flies, aphids, newborn house crickets, and wax moths and their larvae. Give vitamin/mineral supplement regularly.

Behavior: Likes to hide under leaves and woody plants.

IN BRIEF **Class:** *Amphibians* **Order:** *Frogs and toads* **Suborder:** *Modern or advanced frogs* **Family:** *Poison-dart frogs* **Range:** *Guyana to Brazil* **Important:** *Common and scientific names based on native legend that a feather touched to this frog will be dyed a different color.*

Eastern Box Turtle

Terrapene carolina

Terrarium type: 🔺🔺
Level of difficulty: 2
Activity: ☀️
Habit: 🔽 💧

Characteristics: CL up to 6 inches (15 cm). Males somewhat smaller with longer, thicker tail and concave (see page 26) plastron.

Terrarium: Woodland terrarium with bathing dish that is larger than the turtle, with water 2 inches (5 cm) deep. Change water daily. Substrate: sand, soil, peat, 8 inches (20 cm) deep. Provide hiding places. Recommended minimum area of a terrarium (length × width) for housing an adult pair: 32 × 16 inches (80 × 40 cm). Air temperature 75–82.5°F (24–28°C), at night 64°F (18°C), water temperature 64.5–71.5°F (18–22°C), basking islands about 86°F (30°C). Lighting: up to 12 hours. UV radiation required.

Keeping/Care: Keep as a pair and, after testing compatibility, as a group with several females. These turtles burrow in for up to 5 months in winter, depending on their range. Does well in outdoor enclosusres.

Diet: Green plants, fruit, insects, fish, mushrooms, berries, boiled eggs, dry food for aquatic turtles, and vitamin/mineral supplements.

Behavior: Prefers to stay on land. Very alert and curious, likes to dig.

IN BRIEF **Class:** *Reptiles* **Order:** *Tortoises and turtles*
Suborder: *Common-necked or straight-necked turtles*
Family: *Pond and box turtles* **Range:** *Southern Canada to Gulf of Mexico* **Important:** *Locally protected in United States*

Eastern Kingsnake

Lampropeltis getulus getulus

Also: chain kingsnake

Characteristics: TL 40–80 inches (100–200 cm). To ascertain sex, see page 15.

Terrarium type:
Level of difficulty: 1
Activity:
Habit:

Terrarium: Woodland terrarium with hiding places under roots, flat stones, and pieces of cork. Provide climbing branch and large water dish. Recommended terrarium size for 1–2 adults 56 inches (140 cm) long: 56 × 28 × 28 inches (140 × 70 × 70 cm). Air temperature 73.5–77°F (23–25°C), at night 59–68°F (15–20°C), water temperature 64.5–68°F (18–20°C), basking islands 95°F (35°C). Atmospheric humidity 60–80%. Lighting: 12 hours, partly UV.

Keeping/Care: Animals of the same size usually can be kept as a pair if well fed, but cannibalism can occur. Hibernation: 3 months at 50–59°F (10–15°C).

Diet: Mice, rats, chicks, other snakes, lizards, and eggs.

Behavior: In the wild, found in habitats ranging from pine forests through bodies of water, meadows, and fields to mountain slopes. Specimens from northern regions also can be observed in the daytime.

IN BRIEF **Class:** *Reptiles* **Order:** *Scaled reptiles* **Suborder:** *Snakes* **Family:** *Colubrids* **Range:** *Southwestern United States* **Important:** *This subspecies locally protected*

Eastern Ribbon Snake

Thamnophis sauritus sauritus

Characteristics: TL up to 38 inches (100 cm). Females usually larger and more massive. To ascertain sex, see page 15.

Terrarium type:
Level of difficulty: 1
Activity:
Habit:

Terrarium: Woodland terrarium. Large bathing pan, dry basking places, places to hide and climb. Recommended terrarium size for housing an adult pair: 50 × 30 × 20 inches (125 × 75 × 50 cm). For each additional specimen, add 20% to area. Air temperature 77–82.5°F (25–28°C), at night 64.5–71.5°F (18–22°C), water temperature 77°F (25°C), basking islands 86°F (30°C). Values may vary, depending on area of origin. Atmospheric humidity 50–60%. Lighting: 12 hours, partly UV.

Keeping/Care: Quite possible to keep a group of animals of the same size, as they get along well together. Hibernation: 8–12 weeks at 46.5–50°F (8–10°C); specimens from southern range, 4 weeks at 64.5–70°F (18–21°C).

Diet: Earthworms, fish, snails, larger insects such as field crickets, or pinkie mice.

Behavior: Good climber and swimmer.

Similar needs: *Thamnophis proximus*

IN BRIEF **Class:** *Reptiles* **Order:** *Scaled reptiles* **Suborder:** *Snakes* **Family:** *Colubrids* **Range:** *Much of eastern United States, west to Mississippi River*

Emerald Tree Boa

Corallus caninus

Characteristics: TL over 79 inches (200 cm). To ascertain sex, see page 15.

Terrarium: Rainforest terrarium with climbing branches and robust or artificial plants and a large bathing pan. Provide horizontal branches as basking places under a heat lamp. Once a thick branch becomes a regular seat, the snake will seldom leave it. Substrate: leaves, soil, and peat, 8 inches (20 cm) deep. Recommended terrarium size for housing an adult pair: 60 × 40 × 80 inches (150 × 100 × 200 cm). Add 20% for each additional animal. Air temperature 77–86°F (25–30°C), at night 68–77°F (20–25°C), water temperature 77°F (25°C), basking islands 86–95°F (30–35°C). Atmospheric humidity 70–100%. Lighting: 12 hours.

Keeping/Care: Keep as a pair or as a group with only one male. In the rare cases when breeding in captivity is successful, the young are born in the branches and are immediately able to climb.

Diet: Mice, rats, and chicks. Usually accepts only live foods. Sometimes a picky feeder.

Behavior: In the daytime these snakes lie immobile on climbing branches, but when disturbed they are quick to bite.

Terrarium type: 🌿
Level of difficulty: 3
Activity: ☾
Habit: 🌳

IN BRIEF **Class:** *Reptiles* **Order:** *Scaled reptiles*
Suborder: *Snakes* **Family:** *Boas and pythons*
Range: *Colombia to Brazil*

Emperor Scorpion

Pandinus imperator

Characteristics: TL up to 6 inches (15 cm), rarely to 8 inches (20 cm). Males stay somewhat smaller. Females' claws are more pronounced.

Terrarium type: 🏞
Level of difficulty: 1 !
Activity: ☽
Habit: ⬇

Terrarium: Humid woodland terrarium with substrate of sandy soil or woodland soil, 2–4 inches (5–10 cm) deep, covered with leaves and pieces of moss. Keep slightly damp, but prevent standing water. Provide hiding places. Supply shallow water dish. Recommended terrarium size for one adult: 24 × 12 × 12 inches (60 × 30 × 30 cm). Temperature 77–82.5°F (25–28°C), at night 68–75°F (20–24°C), basking islands up to 86°F (30°C). Atmospheric humidity 70–80%. Lighting: 8–10 hours.

Keeping/Care: Keep male or female singly. From October to May, simulate rainy season by misting daily. The sting is only briefly painful, but no more dangerous than a wasp sting. A forest species that requires moisture and humidity.

Diet: Depending on size, house crickets, field crickets, cockroaches, mealworms, beetles, *Zophobas* larvae, and young mice.

Behavior: Peaceful animals. In the wild, they take over air tunnels in termite mounds or dig their own.

IN BRIEF **Class:** *Arachnids* **Order:** *Scorpions*
Suborder: *Neoscorpionina* **Family:** *Scorpionidae*
Range: *Mauritania to Zaire* **Important:** *Slightly poisonous. A good beginner's scorpion.*

European Pond Turtle

Emys orbicularis

Characteristics: CL up to 5 inches (20 cm), depending on subspecies. Males smaller, with concave (see page 26) plastron, thickened tail base, red iris.

Terrarium type: ⌇
Level of difficulty: 1
Activity: ☼
Habit: ◊

Terrarium: Aquatic terrarium with ⅔ water portion. Water level no more than twice the width of the shell. Recommended minimum area (length × width) of a terrarium for housing an adult pair: 40 × 20 inches (100 × 50 cm). Air temperature 77–81°F (25–27°C), at night 64.5–71.5°F (18–22°C), water temperature 73.5–75°F (23–24°C), basking islands about 86°F (30°C). Depending on place of origin, values can be lower or higher. Lighting: 12 hours. UV radiation required.

Keeping/Care: Keep outdoors, if possible. Males get along well together, but the number of females should be larger. Hibernation for northern species 8–12 weeks at 34.5–46.5°F (4–8°C); for southern species, 53.5–59°F (12–15°C).

Diet: Earthworms, crustaceans, fish, and pieces of fish. Also plain gelatin mixture and dry food for aquatic turtles. Vitamin/mineral supplements.

Behavior: Likes to bask in regular spots.

IN BRIEF **Class:** *Reptiles* **Order:** *Tortoises and turtles*
Suborder: *Common-necked or straight-necked turtles*
Family: *Pond and box turtles* **Range:** *Morocco, Tunisia to Lithuania in the north, Iran and Lake Aral region in the east*

False Map Turtle

Graptemys pseudogeographica pseudogeographica

Terrarium type: ⌄
Level of difficulty: 2
Activity: ☀
Habit: ⬤

Characteristics: CL up to 10.7 inches (27 cm). The males are 50% smaller, have a thickened tail base, and have longer claws on the forelegs.

Terrarium: Aquatic terrarium with ⅔ water portion. The water level should be no more than twice the shell width. Recommended minimum area of a terrarium (length × width) for housing an adult pair: 56 × 28 inches (140 × 70 cm). Air temperature 77°F (25°C), at night 68–71.5°F (20–22°C), water temperature 59–81°F (15–27°C), basking islands about 86°F (30°C). Lighting: up to 12 hours. UV radiation required.

Keeping/Care: Needs good water quality. Keep as a pair and, after testing compatibility, as a group with several females. Hibernation: 8–12 weeks at 59°F (15°C).

Diet: Fish, rain worms, crustaceans, and pieces of fish. Also plain gelatin mixture and dry food for aquatic turtles.

Behavior: Relatively shy. Apart from laying eggs, they leave the water only to bask.

IN BRIEF **Class:** *Reptiles* **Order:** *Tortoises and turtles*
Suborder: *Common-necked or straight-necked turtles*
Family: *Pond and box turtles* **Range:** *From the Great Lakes in Canada to the Gulf of Mexico*

Fat-tailed Scorpion

Androctonus australis

Also: Saharan scorpion, yellow fat-tailed scorpion

Terrarium type: 🌵
Level of difficulty: 3 !
Activity: ☽
Habit: ⌣⌣

Characteristics: TL about 3½ inches (8 cm). Female's body is rounder and squatter; females have more pectinal teeth than the smaller males.

Terrarium: Dry desert terrarium with substrate 4 inches (10 cm) deep, mixture of sand and loamy soil. Keep bottom layer slightly damp. Include flat stones and pieces of wood as decorations. Recommended terrarium size for one adult: 12 × 12 × 8 inches (30 × 30 × 20 cm). Temperature 81–86°F (27–30°C), in places 95–104°F (35–40°C), at night 64.5–68°F (18–20°C). Atmospheric humidity 50%. Lighting: 8–10 hours.

Keeping/Care: Because of its toxic venom, the species is emphatically not for beginners. However, it is often commercially available because it is relatively easy to keep and is not very aggressive. Keep male or female singly. To supply with water, mist terrarium lightly every morning.

Diet: House crickets, field crickets, grasshoppers, cockroaches, mealworms, beetles, and *Zophobas* larvae.

Behavior: In the daytime, not to be seen outside its hole.

IN BRIEF **Class:** *Arachnids* **Order:** *Scorpions* **Suborder:** *Neoscorpionina* **Family:** *Thick-tailed scorpions* **Range:** *North Africa* **Important:** *Toxic; beware if you're allergic!*

Fire Salamander

Salamandra salamandra

Characteristics: TL, depending on subspecies, 4¾–11¼ inches (12–28 cm), SVL 2½–5⅜₆ inches (6–13 cm). Males identifiable by enlarged cloacal glands in mating season.

Terrarium type: 🏔️
Level of difficulty: 1
Activity: ☀️ 🌙
Habit: ↙️

Terrarium: Moist woodland terrarium. Substrate: loam and soil on a drainage layer of expanded clay; cover with leaves and moss. Provide pieces of bark, piles of stones, and roots as hiding places. Plant with ferns and ivy. Recommended terrarium size for housing an adult pair: 32 × 14 × 16 inches (80 × 35 × 40 cm). Add 25% to area for each additional specimen. Temperature 64.5–66°F (18–19°C). Temperatures over 68°F (20°C) permissible for only a short time. Atmospheric humidity 80–100%. Lighting: 10–12 hours.

Keeping/Care: Keep animals of equal size as a pair or as a group. Hibernation: 4–5 months at 41.5°F (5°C).

Diet: Slugs, worms, maggots, June bug larvae, caterpillars, and insects.

Behavior: Lives hidden in its cave in the daytime; leaves the hiding place, even during the day, if it rains.

IN BRIEF **Class:** *Amphibians* **Order:** *Salamanders* **Suborder:** *Salamanders and their allies* **Family:** *Salamanders and newts* **Range:** *Algeria, Morocco, southern, central, and eastern Europe to Asia Minor and the Near East*

Fire Skink

Riopa fernandi

Also: *Lygosoma fernandi, Mochlus fernandi*

Characteristics: TL 15¼ inches (38 cm), SVL up to 7¼ inches (18 cm). Hard to sex. Males are usually bigger and more colorful.

Terrarium type:
Level of difficulty: 1
Activity:
Habit:

Terrarium: Woodland terrarium with soil or coconut humus substrate 3¼–4 inches (8–10 cm) deep, suitable for digging. Provide hiding places under flat stone slabs, roots, and pieces of cork. Put plants in pots. Recommended terrarium size for housing an adult pair: 40 × 24 × 20 inches (100 × 60 × 50 cm). Temperature 82.5–90°F (28–32°C), at night 64.5–71.5°F (18–22°C), basking islands 104°F (40°C). Atmospheric humidity 50–70%. Lighting: 12–14 hours. UV radiation required.

Keeping/Care: Keep as a pair or as a group with one male. Hibernation: 6–8 weeks at room temperature.

Diet: Field crickets, house crickets, cockroaches, snails, earthworms, mealworms, young mammals, fish, and green foods.

Behavior: Lives hidden in caves under roots, but quickly becomes tame in a terrarium.

IN BRIEF **Class:** *Reptiles* **Order:** *Scaled reptiles* **Suborder:** *Lizards* **Family:** *Skinks* **Range:** *Western to central Africa*

Fischer's Chameleon

Bradypodion fischeri

Also: *Chamaeleo fischeri*

Characteristics: TL up to 16 inches (40 cm), SVL 7¼–7⅝ inches (18–19 cm). Females ¼ smaller, with smaller horns. Males' dorsal crest ends at the tail, while females' ends between the limbs.

Terrarium type: 🌳
Level of difficulty: 3
Activity: ☼
Habit: 🌳

Terrarium: Woodland terrarium with numerous horizontal branches for climbing. Important: large ventilation areas for adequate fresh air supply. Furnish with plants such as *Ficus benjamina* or *Scindapsus* species. Recommended terrarium size for housing an adult pair: 40 × 24 × 64 inches (100 × 60 × 160 cm). Temperature 71.5–81°F (22–27°C), at night 57.2–64.5°F (14–18°C), basking islands 90°F (32°C). Atmospheric humidity 50–70%, at night 80%. Lighting: 12–14 hours. UV radiation required.

Keeping/Care: Nightly lowering of temperature important to maintain good health. Keep a single specimen; over the long run it is hardly possible to keep a pair. Mist daily to supply the animals with water.

Diet: Varied diet of field crickets, house crickets, cockroaches, grasshoppers, and baby mammals.

Behavior: In the wild, feeds on small lizards.

IN BRIEF **Class:** *Reptiles* **Order:** *Scaled reptiles*
Suborder: *Lizards* **Family:** *Chameleons* **Range:** *Kenya and Tanzania*

Flap-necked Chameleon

Chamaeleo dilepis

Characteristics: TL up to 16¼ inches (42 cm), SVL 7¼–8 inches (18–20 cm). Males have tarsal spur and are about 20% smaller.

Terrarium type: ⟨icon⟩
Level of difficulty: 3
Activity: ⟨icon⟩
Habit: ⟨icon⟩

Terrarium: Semidry terrarium with lots of horizontal climbing branches. Important: large ventilation areas for adequate fresh air supply. Recommended terrarium size for housing an adult pair: 40 × 24 × 64 inches (100 × 60 × 160 cm). Temperature 82.5–86°F (28–30°C), at night 71.5–77°F (22–25°C), basking islands 90°F (32°C). Animals from southern hill regions 71.5–82.5°F (22–28°C), at night 64.5–68°F (18–20°C). Atmospheric humidity 50–60%, at night 80–90%. Lighting: 12–14 hours. UV radiation required.

Keeping/Care: Knowing the regional origin is important because of the large and climatically diverse geographic range. Keep singly, as they are quite aggressive with others of their species. Because these animals do not drink from standing water, install a waterfall or drip system or mist daily.

Diet: Field crickets, house crickets, cockroaches, and young mammals.

Behavior: Lively species. These animals can bite hard when you try to grasp them.

IN BRIEF **Class:** *Reptiles* **Order:** *Scaled reptiles* **Suborder:** *Lizards* **Family:** *Chameleons* **Range:** *Southern half of Africa to Chad in the north*

Flat-tailed House Gecko

Cosymbotus platyurus

Characteristics: TL 4¾ inches (12 cm), SVL up to 2⅜ inches (6 cm). Underside of male's tail is yellow. The species is easily confused with *Hemidactylus fre-natus* (see page 91), but its tail is flatter and broader at the base.

Terrarium type: 🌿
Level of difficulty: 1
Activity: ☀️ 🌙
Habit: 🌳

Terrarium: Rainforest terrarium. Provide rear and side walls suitable for climbing—for example, slabs of cork bark. Vertical bamboo canes up to 1¼ inch (3 cm) thick are ideal for climbing. Substrate: mixture of soil and sand, 1⅝–2 inches (4–5 cm) deep. Provide hiding places among vines and green plants. Recommended terrarium size for housing an adult pair: 14 × 14 × 20 inches (35 × 35 × 50 cm). Add 15% to area for each additional female. Temperature 77–82.5°F (25–28°C), at night 64.5–68°F (18–20°C). Atmospheric humidity 60–80%. Lighting: 12–14 hours. UV radiation required.

Keeping/Care: Keep as a pair or as a group with one male.

Diet: Small to medium-sized house crickets and field crickets, as well as flies, wax moths, and meadow plankton.

Behavior: In the wild, these agile climbers are often quite sedentary. Often found on walls and house walls.

IN BRIEF **Class:** *Reptiles* **Order:** *Scaled reptiles*
Suborder: *Lizards* **Family:** *Geckos* **Range:** *India, Southeast Asia to New Guinea*

Flying Gecko

Ptychozoon kuhli

Characteristics: TL 8 inches (20 cm), SVL 4½ inches (11 cm). Males identifiable by the distinct preanal pores (see page 27).

Terrarium type: 🌿
Level of difficulty: 1
Activity: ☀ ☾
Habit: 🌳

Terrarium: Rainforest terrarium with cork rear wall for climbing. Possibly also cover side walls with cork. Provide branches for climbing and places to hide. Keep moisture-retaining substrate— such as sphagum/peat or humus—slightly moist. Recommended terrarium size for housing an adult pair: 20 × 20 × 28 inches (50 × 50 × 70 cm). Temperature 75–82.5°F (24–28°C), at night 68–71.5°F (20–22°C), basking islands 86°F (30°C). Atmospheric humidity 80–90%. Lighting: 10 hours.

Keeping/Care: Keep as a pair, or keep one male with several females. Hibernation: 6–8 weeks at 50°F (10°C).

Diet: Field crickets, house crickets, wax moths and their larvae, moths, and meadow plankton.

Behavior: In the daytime, scarcely visible when camouflaged against the trunks of trees. When jumping or dropping, it spreads its webbed toes and tail fringe so that it actually glides to the ground.

IN BRIEF   Class: *Reptiles* **Order:** *Scaled reptiles*
Suborder: *Lizards* **Family:** *Geckos* **Range:** *Indochina to Thailand, Malaysia, and Indonesia*

Four-toed Salamander

Hemidactylium scutatum

Characteristics: TL 3⅝–4 inches (9–10 cm), SVL 1⅝ inches (4 cm). Males around ¼ smaller. Only four toes on each foot. Can discard its tail if threatened.

Terrarium type: ◡◠
Level of difficulty: 1
Activity: ☼ ☽
Habit: ⬇⬇ ◯

Terrarium: Bog-like woodland terrarium with ⅓ shallow water portion. Flat transition to land portion. Substrate: 4¾–6¾ inches (12–17 cm) deep, made of soil, humus or peat/sphagnum moss mixture covered with pieces of bark, decayed branches, leaves, and moss. Recommended terrarium size for housing an adult pair: 16 × 12 × 12 inches (40 × 30 × 30 cm). Add 25% to area for each additional specimen. Air and water temperature for northern species 63–70°F (17–21°C), for southern species 68–71.5°F (20–22°C), at night slightly cooler. Atmospheric humidity 80–100%. Lighting: 10 hours.

Keeping/Care: Keep animals of the same size as a group. Hibernation: for northern subspecies, 8–10 weeks at 41.5–46.5°F (5–8°C); for southern subspecies, at 50–53.5°F (10–12°C).

Diet: Snails, caterpillars, maggots, small June bug larvae, and insects.

Behavior: Lives under stones, moss, and wood near bodies of water. Lays eggs on land; the larvae reach the water by wriggling.

IN BRIEF **Class:** *Amphibians* **Order:** *Salamanders* **Suborder:** *Salamanders and their allies* **Family:** *Lungless salamanders* **Range:** *Great Lakes region south to southeastern United States*

Frilled Lizard

Chlamydosaurus kingii

Characteristics: TL 32 inches (95 cm), SVL 11¼ inches (28 cm). Females stay smaller. Up to age of 3 months, males can be identified by the hemipenes sacs; after that by the thickening of the tail bases.

Terrarium type: 🖾🖾
Level of difficulty: 3
Activity: ☼
Habit: 🌳

Terrarium: Forest terrarium with gravel substrate 2 inches (5 cm) deep. Provide lots of branches for climbing; they can be decorated with artificial plants. Recommended terrarium size for housing an adult pair: 48 × 40 × 80 inches (120 × 100 × 200 cm). Temperature 86–100°F (30–38°C), at night 64.5–71.5°F (18–22°C), basking islands 104–113°F (40–45°C). Atmospheric humidity 50–70%. Up to 14 hours of lighting. UV radiation required.

Keeping/Care: Keep as a pair or as a group with one male. Hibernation: 6–8 weeks at 64.5–68°F (18–20°C).

Diet: Field crickets, house crickets, cockroaches, caterpillars, and beetles. Feed in moderation, since these animals gain weight quickly. Vitamin/mineral supplementation is important.

Behavior: Not very active. When threatened, displays its frill as a deterrent. On the ground, these agamas run on their hind legs when fleeing.

IN BRIEF **Class:** *Reptiles* **Order:** *Scaled reptiles* **Suborder:** *Lizards* **Family:** *Agamas* **Range:** *Northeastern Australia and southern New Guinea*

Giant Desert Hairy Scorpion

Hadrurus arizonensis

Terrarium type: 🌵
Level of difficulty: 2 !
Activity: ☽
Habit: ⊻⊻

Characteristics: TL up to 5⅝ inches (14 cm). As a rule, male has larger pectines and more pectinal teeth.

Terrarium: Dry desert terrarium with substrate 4–8 inches (10–20 cm) deep, a mixture of sand and terrarium soil. Add stones and pieces of wood as decorations. Provide a shallow water dish. Recommended terrarium size for one adult: 12 × 8 × 12 inches (30 × 20 × 30 cm). Temperature 77–86°F (25–30°C), at night 59–68°F (15–20°C). Atmospheric humidity 40%. Lighting: 8–10 hours.

Keeping/Care: Keep a male or a female singly. Do not mist. This scorpion's sting is painful only for a short time but causes slight swelling and reddening.

Diet: Field crickets, cockroaches, mealworms, and beetles.

Behavior: Lively, not very aggressive species that digs burrows in the substrate to live in.

IN BRIEF **Class:** *Arachnids* **Order:** *Scorpions*
Suborder: *Neoscorpionina* **Family:** *Hairy scorpions*
Range: *Deserts of southwestern United States to Mexico*
Important: *Be careful when you reach into the aquarium, because this species can hurl its venom for a distance of several centimeters. Can live over 15 years.*

Giant Leaf Insect

Phyllium giganteum

Characteristics: TL up to 4½ inches (11 cm). Males have longer antennae and wings that are broadened at the base.

Terrarium type: 🎋
Level of difficulty: 1
Activity: ☽
Habit: 🌳

Terrarium: Woodland terrarium. Use humus, peat, or terrarium soil as substrate. Food plants placed in heavy containers can serve as climbing branches. Rear wall of coarse cork bark. Recommended terrarium size for 3–4 adults: 12 × 16 × 16 inches (30 × 40 × 40 cm). Temperature 79–86°F (26–30°C), at night 71.5–77°F (22–25°C). Atmospheric humidity 70–80%. Lighting: 10–12 hours.

Keeping/Care: Cover made of wire mesh is important for ventilation and to prevent buildup of condensation because the larvae will adhere to it and die. If fed oak leaves, more specimens are known to survive; juveniles often reject blackberry leaves. To ensure food supply in winter, plant acorns or feed animals evergreen oaks or *Pyracantha* (fire-thorn).

Diet: Various leaves: oak, blackberry, raspberry, rose, hawthorn, beech, and rhododendron.

Behavior: Nonsexual reproduction without males possible (virgin birth or parthenogenesis).

IN BRIEF **Class:** *Insects* **Order:** *Stick and leaf insects* **Family:** *Leaf insects* **Range:** *Western Malaysia*

Giant Prickly Stick Insect

Extatosoma tiaratum

Also: Macleay's spectre, Australian spiny leaf insect

Terrarium type: 🔼🔼
Level of difficulty: 1
Activity: ☽
Habit: 🌳

Characteristics: TL of females up to 5⅝ inches (14 cm); they have tiny spines on their bodies and very short wings. Males are ⅓ smaller, slimmer, with wings that cover the abdomen.

Terrarium: Woodland terrarium with slightly damp substrate of humus, peat/sphagum moss mixture, or terrarium soil, 1¼–2 inches (3–5 cm) deep. Don't keep the top layer so wet that the animals' balls of feces mildew. Food plants placed in heavy containers can provide branches for climbing. Rear wall made of coarse cork bark. Recommended terrarium size for up to 6 adult specimens: 16 × 12 × 16 inches (40 × 30 × 40 cm). Temperature 68–77°F (20–25°C), at night 64.5–68°F (18–20°C). Atmospheric humidity 50–70%. Lighting: 10–12 hours.

Keeping/Care: Make sure the terrarium is well ventilated; ideally, use wire mesh as lid. Undemanding species.

Diet: Various leaves: blackberry, raspberry, rose, hawthorn, oak, beech, and rhododendron.

Behavior: Can reproduce without males, though only females will result from the unfertilized eggs.

IN BRIEF **Class:** *Insects* **Order:** *Stick and leaf insects* **Family:** *Leaf insects* **Range:** *Northern Australia and New Guinea*

Giant Whiteknee Tarantula

Acanthoscurria geniculata

Characteristics: Body up to 3⁹⁄₁₆ inches (9 cm). Adult males lack the stripes typical of females' limbs.

Terrarium: Rainforest terrarium with substrate about 4 inches (10 cm) deep, mixture of peat and loam. Keep half of substrate moist. Decorate with roots and artificial plants. Supply water container. Recommended terrarium size for one adult: 16 × 12 × 12 inches (40 × 30 × 30 cm). Temperature 75–82.5°F (24–28°C), at night 68–71.5°F (20–22°C). Atmospheric humidity 70–80%. Lighting: 8–10 hours.

Keeping/Care: Keep male or female singly.

Diet: Depending on size, flies, house crickets, grasshoppers, small lizards and frogs, and pinkie mice.

Behavior: Ground-dwelling species. Often can be observed in daytime as well. These tarantulas dig holes into which they retreat only when threatened or for eating or molting. Some individuals react quite aggressively when disturbed; they defend themselves by biting or flicking urticating hairs (see page 20). Be careful.

Terrarium type:
Level of difficulty: 2 !
Activity:
Habit:

IN BRIEF   **Class:** *Arachnids* **Order:** *Spiders*
Suborder: *Tarantulas and relatives* **Family:** *Tarantulas*
Range: *Southern Venezuela to northern Brazil*

Gold Dust Day Gecko

Phelsuma laticauda

Characteristics: TL 5⅝ inches (14 cm), SVL 3 inches (7.5 cm). Males identifiable from age of about one year by clearly visible preanofemoral pores (see page 27).

Terrarium type: 🗻
Level of difficulty: 1
Activity: ☼
Habit: 🌳

Terrarium: Woodland terrarium. Furnish with smooth-leaved plants and smooth branches for climbing. Provide hiding places. Recommended terrarium size for housing an adult pair: 16 × 16 × 24 inches (40 × 40 × 60 cm). Add 15% to area for each additional female. Temperature 79–90°F (26–32°C), at night 70–75°F (21–24°C). Atmospheric humidity 50–60%, at night 80–90%. Lighting: 10–12 hours. UV radiation required.

Keeping/Care: Keep as a pair or as a group with one male. If captive-bred animals are kept warmer than recommended, they tend to become weakened and are permanently impaired.

Diet: Field crickets, house crickets, and wax moths and their larvae. Once a week, mashed fruit. Calcium for forming the hard-shelled eggs is especially important.

Behavior: In the wild, found on banana plants, palms, walls, and even in houses.

IN BRIEF **Class:** *Reptiles* **Order:** *Scaled reptiles* **Suborder:** *Lizards* **Family:** *Geckos* **Range:** *Madagascar, Comoros islands Mayotte and Anjouan, islands Farquhar and Cerf*

Golden Gecko

Gecko ulikovski

Characteristics: TL up to 12 inches (30 cm), SVL up to 5⅒ inches (13 cm). Females stay smaller, have shorter, narrower heads. Males have prominent hemipenes sacs (see page 26).

Terrarium type:	
Level of difficulty: 1	
Activity:	
Habit:	

Terrarium: Rainforest terrarium. Bamboo for climbing, hiding places in plants, and places to sleep behind pieces of cork placed upright. Moisture-retaining substrate. Recommended terrarium size for housing an adult pair: 32 × 32 × 40 inches (80 × 80 × 100 cm). Add 15% to area for each additional female. Temperature 77–82.5°F (25–28°C), at night 68–71.5°F (20–22°C). Atmospheric humidity 70–85%. Lighting: 10–12 hours.

Keeping/Care: Keep as a pair or as a group with only one male. Some individuals learn to drink from the water bowl, but be sure to mist regularly.

Diet: House crickets, cockroaches, field crickets, and grasshoppers. Mashed fruit is sometimes accepted.

Behavior: Some are active in the daytime as well. Quite shy initially. They leave their climbing branches only to hunt.

IN BRIEF **Class:** *Reptiles* **Order:** *Scaled reptiles* **Suborder:** *Lizards* **Family:** *Geckos* **Range:** *Vietnam*

Golden Mantella

Mantella aurantiaca

Characteristics: SVL up to 1 inch (2.5 cm). Males somewhat smaller and slimmer, with a darker throat, as well as pads on the inner surface of the thighs and in the cloacal region.

Terrarium type: 🌿
Level of difficulty: 2
Activity: ☀
Habit: 🔽

Terrarium: Rainforest terrarium with 1¼-inch (3-cm) water level. Provide a sloping bank made of peat slabs and lots of little hiding places. Recommended terrarium size for 3 adults: 20 × 16 × 20 inches (50 × 40 × 50 cm). Temperature 64.5–71.5°F (18–22°C), at night 53.5–61°F (12–16°C). Water temperature by day 71.5°F (22°C), at night 61–66°F (16–19°C). Atmospheric humidity 80–90%, at night up to 100%, from July to September 20% less. Low lighting: 12–14 hours in summer, 10 hours in winter.

Keeping/Care: Quite susceptible to stress. Keep at least 2 males per female.

Diet: Fruit flies, aphids, and small insects no larger than house-flies. These animals prefer to hunt prey in the morning hours.

Behavior: Males wrestle together, but don't hurt each other. Hard to breed. Commercially available specimens usually captured in the wild.

IN BRIEF **Class:** *Amphibians* **Order:** *Frogs and toads* **Suborder:** *Modern or advanced frogs* **Family:** *Old World tree frogs* **Range:** *Toroto-Sotsy swamps in Madagascar*

Golden Tegu

Tupinambis teguixin

Terrarium type:	🌵
Level of difficulty:	2
Activity:	☀️
Habit:	⩗

Also: *Colombian tegu*

Characteristics: TL up to 44 inches (110 cm), SVL 14 inches (35 cm). Females 10–15% smaller. Males have broader heads, thickened tail base, and larger femoral pores (see page 26).

Terrarium: Rainforest terrarium. Substrate, 8–12 inches (20–30 cm) deep, of slightly damp sand and loam, in which these animals can dig their caves. Provide roots and pieces of cork as hiding places. Recommended terrarium size for housing an adult pair: 88 × 64 × 60 inches (220 × 160 × 150 cm). Temperature 77–86°F (25–30°C), at night 71.5–75°F (22–24°C), basking islands 95°F (35°C). Atmospheric humidity 60–80%. Lighting: 12–14 hours. UV radiation required.

Keeping/Care: Keep as a pair or as a group with one male. Supply water by daily misting, but include a water dish as well.

Diet: Mice, rats, chicks, eggs, fish, and meat. Some fruit.

Behavior: Loves the sun. Good swimmer and diver.

IN BRIEF **Class:** *Reptiles* **Order:** *Scaled reptiles* **Suborder:** *Lizards* **Family:** *Whiptail lizards and their allies (tegus)* **Range:** *Tropical rainforests, northern South America, and Amazonian Peru*

Goliath Tarantula

Theraphosa blondi

Also: Goliath birdeater

Characteristics: Body up to 4 inches (10 cm). Males smaller and darker with enlarged pedipalps.

Terrarium type: 🌿
Level of difficulty: 3 !
Activity: ☽
Habit: ⬇⬇

Terrarium: Rainforest terrarium. Cork-bark caves with diameter of about 8 inches (20 cm) as hiding places. Water container essential. Recommended terrarium size for one adult: 24 × 16 × 16 inches (60 × 40 × 40 cm). Temperature 77–82.5°F (25–28°C), at night 68–73.5°F (20–23°C). Atmospheric humidity 80–90%. Lighting: 8–10 hours.

Keeping/Care: Keep male or female singly. Be careful when working on the terrarium, as the species is unpredictable and can inflict a painful, but not serious bite. Fangs can reach 1 inch (2.5 cm) in length! Don't keep the substrate too dry, as these tarantulas quickly become dehydrated, but avoid excessive sogginess, to which they are very sensitive.

Diet: Depending on size, flies, house crickets, lizards, frogs, and grasshoppers; baby mice.

Behavior: In the daytime, the species buries itself in rodents' burrows, closing the entrance by spinning a web.

IN BRIEF   Class: *Arachnids* **Order:** *Spiders*
   Suborder: *Tarantulas and relatives* **Family:** *Tarantulas*
   Range: *Venezuela, French Guyana to northern Brazil*
   Important: *The largest species of spider.*

Gray Tree Frog

Hyla versicolor

Also: Eastern gray tree frog, common gray tree frog

Characteristics: SVL up to 2½ inches (6 cm). Males slightly slimmer, with dark gray, wrinkled throat.

Terrarium type: 🌿
Level of difficulty: 1
Activity: ☀ ☾
Habit: 🌳

Terrarium: Woodland terrarium with a water bowl for soaking. Provide rear wall made of cork and climbing aids in the form of branches. Recommended terrarium size for housing an adult pair: 16 × 16 × 24 inches (40 × 40 × 60 cm). For northern specimens, daytime temperature 64.5–75°F (18–24°C), at night 61–64.5°F (16–18°C), for southern specimens, 75–82.5°F (24–28°C) by day, at night 64.5–68°F (18–20°C). Atmospheric humidity 50–70%. Lighting: 10–12 hours.

Keeping/Care: These frogs get along well together. Hibernation: 8–12 weeks at 50–59°F (10–15°C).

Diet: House crickets, grasshoppers, field crickets, flies, and wax moths.

Behavior: Barely visible in the daytime on tree bark covered with gray lichen.

Similar needs: *Hyla chrysoscelis*

IN BRIEF   Class: *Amphibians* **Order:** *Frogs and toads*
Suborder: *Modern or advanced frogs* **Family:** *New World tree frogs* **Range:** *Midwestern to southeastern United States*

Green and Black Poison-Dart Frog

Dendrobates auratus

Terrarium type: 🌿
Level of difficulty: 2
Activity: ☀
Habit:

Characteristics: SVL 1⅝ inches (4 cm). Males somewhat smaller, most readily identifiable by their territorial fighting.

Terrarium: Rainforest terrarium with 20% water portion. Substrate: peat/soil mix or forest soil. Use coconut shells as places to hide or to lay eggs. Recommended terrarium size for one adult breeding pair: 20 × 16 × 20 inches (50 × 40 × 50 cm). Increase area by 50% for breeding group of up to 4 specimens. Temperature 75–79°F (24–26°C), at night 68–75°F (20–24°C). Lighting: 12–14 hours.

Keeping/Care: Keep as a pair or as a group with one male and 2–3 females—no more, as they are aggressive toward each other. Because crossbreeding can occur, do not keep with *D. tinctorius* (see page 107) and *D. leucomelas* (see page 64).

Diet: Fruit flies, houseflies, aphids, and wax moths and their larvae. Vitamins and mineral supplements regularly.

Behavior: In the wild, these animals live near large trees, under large heaps of leaves, and on herbaceous plants and shrubs near the ground.

IN BRIEF **Class:** *Amphibians* **Order:** *Frogs and toads* **Suborder:** *Modern or advanced frogs* **Family:** *Poison-dart frogs* **Range:** *Nicaragua to Panama*

Green Anole

Anolis carolinensis

Characteristics: TL 8⅜ inches (21 cm), SVL up to 2⅞ inches (7 cm). Males are bigger, about 1⅝ inches (4 cm) longer (TL), and can be identified by their red throat sacs.

Terrarium type:
Level of difficulty: 1
Activity:
Habit:

Terrarium: Woodland terrarium with lots of places to climb and plantings. Recommended terrarium size for housing an adult pair: 16 × 16 × 24 inches (40 × 40 × 60 cm). Temperature 82.5–86°F (28–30°C), at night 68–71.5°F (20–22°C), basking islands 86°F (30°C). Atmospheric humidity 60–65%, at night 80%. Lighting: 12–14 hours. UV radiation required.

Keeping/Care: Keep as a pair or in groups with one male. In winter, you may lower temperature to 64.5–68°F (18–20°C) and reduce lighting period to 8 hours, but this is not required.

Diet: Flies, house crickets, and wax moths. These lizards reject some food types for a while. Some individuals choose to fast from October to March, even without lowered temperatures.

Behavior: The species remains shy. When courting, or declaring its territory, males extend their dark-red to violet throat fans and bob up and down. Depending on mood or temperature, can be either green or brown in color.

IN BRIEF **Class:** *Reptiles* **Order:** *Scaled reptiles* **Suborder:** *Lizards* **Family:** *Iguanas* **Range:** *Much of southeastern United States, Cuba, Bahamas, Florida, introduced in California*

135

Green Basilisk

Basiliscus plumifrons

Characteristics: TL 26–28 inches (65–70 cm), SVL 6⅞–9⅜ inches (17–24 cm). Males have high fins on back and dorsal edge of tail.

Terrarium type:
Level of difficulty: 2
Activity:
Habit:

Terrarium: Rainforest terrarium. Large water tank at least twice the length of the SVL. Water level of 4¾–5¹³⁄₁₆ inches (12–13 cm). Change water often. Decorate with vertical and horizontal climbing branches the thickness of an arm. Recommended terrarium size for housing an adult pair 28 inches (70 cm) long: 80 × 40 × 80 inches (200 × 100 × 200 cm). Air temperature 77–86°F (25–30°C), at night 68–71.5°F (20–22°C), water temperature 77°F (25°C), basking islands 104°F (40°C). Atmospheric humidity 70–90%. Lighting: 12–14 hours. UV radiation required.

Keeping/Care: Keep as a pair or in groups with one male. This species needs no hibernation period, but can be kept drier for a good 3–4 months.

Diet: Field crickets, house crickets, wax moths, *Zophobas* larvae, young mice, and vitamin/mineral supplementation.

Behavior: Excellent climbers, good swimmers and runners, across water as well. Pronounced flight behavior.

IN BRIEF **Class:** *Reptiles* **Order:** *Scaled reptiles* **Suborder:** *Lizards* **Family:** *Iguanas* **Range:** *Guatemala to Costa Rica*

Green Cat Snake

Boiga cyanea

Also: Blue-chinned green cat-eyed snake

Terrarium type: 🌿
Level of difficulty: 3 !
Activity: 🌄 🌙
Habit: 🌳

Characteristics: TL up to 64 inches (160 cm), rarely to 80 inches (200 cm).

Terrarium: Rainforest terrarium with slightly damp substrate, 2–4 inches (5–10 cm) deep. Include large pan for bathing. Furnish with climbing branches of various diameters. Provide cork tube as hiding place. Plant terrarium with vines and bromeliads. Recommended terrarium size for one adult: 64 × 72 × 64 inches (160 × 180 × 160 cm). Air temperature 79–82.5°F (26–28°C), at night 61–68°F (16–20°C), water temperature 64.5–71.5°F (18–22°C), basking islands 86°F (30°C). Atmospheric humidity 70–80%. Lighting: 10–12 hours.

Keeping/Care: Advisable to keep singly because of cannibalism. The venom has little effect on humans.

Diet: Mice and rats of appropriate size, chicks.

Behavior: Hides in the daytime in dense plantings or in hollow trees.

IN BRIEF **Class:** *Reptiles* **Order:** *Scaled reptiles* **Suborder:** *Snakes* **Family:** *Colubrids* **Range:** *Indochina, Myanmar, Thailand, Laos, Cambodia, Vietnam to China and Malaysia* **Important:** *Mildly venomous. Keeping poisonous snakes is prohibited or subject to the granting of a permit in many parts of the United States.*

Green Iguana

Iguana iguana

Terrarium type:
Level of difficulty: 1
Activity:
Habit:

Characteristics: TL 40–80 inches (100–200 cm), SVL 12–14 inches (30–35 cm). Males slightly larger, with prominent dorsal crest and throat sac, as well as femoral pores (see page 26).

Terrarium: Woodland or rainforest terrarium. Sand and humus substrate, kept slightly damp. Water receptacle, as these lizards enjoy bathing. Half of the climbing branches should be thicker than the lizards' bodies. Good air circulation, with no drafts, is important. Recommended terrarium size for housing an adult pair: at least 110 × 66 × 80 inches (275 × 165 × 200 cm). Temperature 77–95°F (25–35°C), at night 71.5–77°F (22–25°C), basking islands 113°F (45°C). Atmospheric humidity 60–90%. Lighting: 14 hours. UV radiation required.

Keeping/Care: Keep as a single specimen or group with only one male. Because so much space is needed, the species is recommended only for conscientious terrarium keepers with enough room!

Diet: Mainly leafy plants, sprouts, and herbs. Vegetables such as cucumbers and tomatoes. Rarely, fruits. Vitamin/mineral supplements.

Behavior: In the wild, these lizards prefer to stay near water.

IN BRIEF **Class:** *Reptiles* **Order:** *Scaled reptiles*
Suborder: *Lizards* **Family:** *Iguanas* **Range:** *Southern Mexico to southern Brazil*

Green Lizard

Lacerta viridis

Terrarium type: 🌲🌲
Level of difficulty: 1
Activity: ☀
Habit: 🌱

Characteristics: TL 16 inches (40 cm), SVL up to 4¾ inches (12 cm). Males have thickened tail base and are more brilliantly colored.

Terrarium: Woodland terrarium. Good ventilation required. Provide climbing walls and branches, as well as hiding places such as cork tubes and large stones. Suitable substrate: soil layer about 2–4 inches (5–10 cm) deep, including some sand and gravel. Furnish with potted plants. Recommended terrarium size for housing an adult pair: 40 × 24 × 24 inches (100 × 60 × 60 cm). Temperature 77–86°F (25–30°C), at night 61–68°F (16–20°C), basking islands 95–104°F (35–40°C). Atmospheric humidity 60–70%. Lighting: 10–12 hours. UV radiation required.

Keeping/Care: Keep as a pair or as a group with only one male. Hibernation: 8–12 weeks at 46.5–50°F (8–10°C).

Diet: Grasshoppers, house crickets, field crickets, cockroaches, earthworms, and mealworms. Adult specimens occasionally eat young mice as well. Sweet fruit is accepted.

Behavior: Predominantly ground-dwelling, but is an excellent climber.

IN BRIEF **Class:** *Reptiles* **Order:** *Scaled reptiles*
Suborder: *Lizards* **Family:** *Wall lizards* **Range:** *Central, southern, and eastern Europe to Asia Minor*

Green Sailfin Dragon

Hydrosaurus weberi

Also: Weber's sailfin lizard

Characteristics: TL up to 56 inches (140 cm), SVL 15¼ inches (38 cm). Males slightly larger, with taller crests and darker markings on head and limbs.

Terrarium type: 🌿
Level of difficulty: 3
Activity: ☀
Habit: 🌳

Terrarium: Roomy rainforest terrarium. Water portion ⅓ to ½ of area. Water depth 12–24 inches (30–60 cm). Provide lots of climbing branches as well as hiding places. Plant with tough or artificial plants. Recommended terrarium size for housing an adult pair: 80 × 48 × 72 inches (200 × 120 × 180 cm). Air temperature 77–90°F (25–32°C), at night 64.5–71.5°F (18–22°C), water temperature 77°F (25°C), basking islands 104–113°F (40–45°C). Atmospheric humidity 70%. Lighting: up to 14 hours. UV radiation required.

Keeping/Care: Because of susceptibility to stress and feeding problems, the species has acquired a bad reputation. Wild-caught animals frequently heavily parasitized. Keep as a pair or as a group with one male. Hibernation: 8–10 weeks at 59°F (15°C).

Diet: Field crickets, house crickets, cockroaches, *Zophobas* larvae, baby rodents. Also fruit, leaves, and green leaf lettuce. Add vitamin/mineral supplements.

Behavior: Pronounced flight behavior.

IN BRIEF **Class:** *Reptiles* **Order:** *Scaled reptiles* **Suborder:** *Lizards* **Family:** *Agamas* **Range:** *Philippines, Indonesia to New Guinea*

Green Spiny Lizard

Sceloporus malachiticus

Also: Spiny lizard, green lizard, scorpion lizard, emerald swift

Characteristics: TL 8 inches (20 cm), SVL 3¼ inches (8 cm) or larger. Males more colorful, somewhat larger, with wider head and thickened tail base.

Terrarium: Woodland terrarium with climbing branches and rear wall that can be climbed. On the ground, provide hiding places under pieces of cork or stone slabs. Sandy substrate, kept mostly dry, but with one part slightly damp. Provide a shallow water dish. Recommended terrarium size for housing an adult pair: 40 × 20 × 28 inches (100 × 50 × 70 cm). Temperature 77–86°F (25–30°C), at night 59–68°F (15–20°C), basking islands 95°F (35°C). Atmospheric humidity 50–80%. Lighting: 14 hours. UV radiation required.

Keeping/Care: Keep as a pair or as a group with only one male, as males are very quarrelsome and territorial.

Diet: House crickets, cockroaches, field crickets, grasshoppers, wax moths and their larvae, baby rodents. Now and then, leaves and flowers.

Behavior: Lives in tropical mountain forests. Live-bearing.

Terrarium type:
Level of difficulty: 1
Activity:
Habit:

IN BRIEF **Class:** *Reptiles* **Order:** *Scaled reptiles* **Suborder:** *Lizards* **Family:** *Iguanas* **Range:** *Southern Mexico to Panama*

Green Tree Frog

Hyla cinerea

Also: American green tree frog

Characteristics: SVL up to 2¾ inches (7 cm). Males 20% smaller, with green throat and large, wrinkled skin on throat.

Terrarium type: 🌿
Level of difficulty: 1
Activity: ☀ ☾
Habit: 🌳

Terrarium: Woodland terrarium with water dish for soaking. Water level 2 inches (5 cm). Provide places to hide and climb. Decorate abundantly with stable, large-leaved plants. Recommended terrarium size for housing an adult pair: 16 × 16 × 24 inches (40 × 40 × 60 cm). Temperature 71.5–82.5°F (22–28°C), at night 63–68°F (17–20°C). Atmospheric humidity 60–80%. Lighting: 10–12 hours.

Keeping/Care: These animals get along well together. Install a small heat lamp; in the daytime the frogs sometimes enjoy staying under its beam. Hibernation: 6–8 weeks at 46.5–50°F (8–10°C), with a 2-week transition period at 61–68°F (16–20°C) without food.

Diet: House crickets, grasshoppers, field crickets, flies, and wax moths.

Behavior: Sleeps during the day in shady places, such as the undersides of leaves (clinging there by means of adhesive discs).

IN BRIEF **Class:** *Amphibians* **Order:** *Frogs and toads*
Suborder: *Modern or advanced frogs* **Family:** *New World tree frogs* **Range:** *Southeastern United States*

Green Tree Python

Morelia viridis

Also: previously *Chondropython viridis*
Characteristics: TL up to 80 inches
(200 cm). To ascertain sex, see page 15.
Terrarium: Rainforest terrarium with
bathing tank that takes up 25% of the area. Stable tree with horizontal branches for climbing and resting, robust plants such as
philodendrons. Recommended terrarium size for housing an
adult pair: 60 × 40 × 80 inches (150 × 100 × 200 cm). For each
additional specimen, add 20% to area. Air temperature 77–86°F
(25–30°C), at night 68–77°F (20–25°C), water temperature 77°F
(25°C), basking islands 95°F (35°C). Atmospheric humidity
70–80%. Lighting: 12 hours.
Keeping/Care: Keep as a single animal, a pair, in groups with only
one male, or in groups of females only. Males do not get along
together. These animals are quick to feel threatened, and young snakes
in particular tend to strike. The species as a whole is considered rather
aggressive. Their long teeth can produce a painful and nasty bite.
Diet: Mice, rats, and chicks. Usually only live animals are con-
sumed. Sometimes these snakes are picky feeders and require
proper food presentation.
Behavior: Rarely comes to the ground.

Terrarium type:
Level of difficulty: 3
Activity:
Habit:

IN BRIEF **Class:** *Reptiles* **Order:** *Scaled reptiles*
Suborder: *Snakes* **Family:** *Boas and pythons*
Range: *Northern Australia to New Guinea*

Guatemalan Redrump Tarantula

Brachypelma sabulosum

Also: *Brachypelma sp. Guatemala*

Characteristics: Body up to 2⅜ inches (7 cm). Semen sacs can be seen in the softened cast-off skin of the female's abdomen.

Terrarium type: [icon]
Level of difficulty: 1 !
Activity: [icon]
Habit: [icon]

Terrarium: Rainforest terrarium with substrate of leaf mold or humus, at least 2 inches (5 cm) deep, kept damp, but not wet, in one corner. Provide cork tube with diameter of about 6 inches (15 cm) as hiding place. Supply water container. Recommended terrarium size for one adult: 12 × 16 × 12 inches (30 × 40 × 30 cm). Temperature 75–82.5°F (24–28°C), at night 64.5–71.5°F (18–22°C). Atmospheric humidity 70–80%. Lighting: 8–10 hours.

Keeping/Care: Keep male or female singly. Keep substrate merely damp; the species is sensitive to standing water. It will retreat when you are working on the terrarium. Easy to breed.

Diet: Depending on size, flies, house crickets, grasshoppers, and baby mammals.

Behavior: Peaceful ground dweller; when threatened, would rather flee than flick hairs (see page 20). Predominantly nocturnal, sometimes diurnal.

IN BRIEF **Class:** *Arachnids* **Order:** *Spiders*
Suborder: *Tarantulas and relatives* **Family:** *Tarantulas*
Range: *Northern Guatemala*

Haitian Brown Tarantula

Phormictopus cancerides

Terrarium type:	
Level of difficulty: 3 !	
Activity:	
Habit:	

Characteristics: Body up to 3¼ inches (8 cm). In the softened cast-off skin of the female's abdomen, the semen storage sacs are clearly visible.

Terrarium: Humid woodland terrarium. Substrate: about 2 inches (5 cm) deep, soil and sand covered with leaves and moss; keep only slightly moist. Provide caves in the form of cork bark, with diameter of about 6 inches (15 cm). Supply shallow water dish. Recommended terrarium size for one adult: 16 × 12 × 12 inches (40 × 30 × 30 cm). Temperature 71.5–79°F (22–26°C), at night 64.5–68°F (18–20°C). Atmospheric humidity 80%. Lighting: 8–10 hours.

Keeping/Care: Sensitive to standing water; ventilate terrarium well as preventive measure. Keep male or female singly. Perform tasks in the terrarium with great care, as the species is quick to flick hairs in self-defense (see page 20) and bite. Its bite is very painful and considered potentially dangerous to humans.

Diet: Depending on size, wax moths, house crickets, field crickets, cockroaches, and baby mammals.

Behavior: Digs cavities in the ground. These highly aggressive animals attack everything that moves. Use extreme care in terrarium maintenance.

IN BRIEF **Class:** *Arachnids* **Order:** *Spiders* **Suborder:** *Tarantulas and relatives* **Family:** *Tarantulas* **Range:** *Haiti and Dominican Republic* **Important:** *If you're allergic, take care!*

Helmeted Basilisk

Corytophanes cristatus

Characteristics: TL 14 inches (35 cm), SVL 4¾ inches (12 cm). Male bigger, with larger throat sacs and helmets, as well as thickened tail base.

Terrarium type: ▨
Level of difficulty: 1
Activity: ☼
Habit: ♧

Terrarium: Rainforest terrarium with lots of branches for climbing and large water container. Plants such as *Ficus benjamina*. Substrate: soil/peat mixture or bark. Keep terrarium well ventilated to prevent standing water. Recommended terrarium size for housing an adult pair: 28 × 20 × 40 inches (70 × 50 × 100 cm). Temperature 75–86°F (24–30°C), at night 64.5–68°F (18–20°C), basking islands 95–104°F (35–40°C). Atmospheric humidity 90–100%. Lighting: 12–14 hours. UV radiation required.

Keeping/Care: Keep as a pair or as a group with only one male. Wild-caught specimens have trouble adapting to terrarium life.

Diet: Field crickets, grasshoppers, cockroaches, wax moths and their larvae, and baby mammals.

Behavior: Peaceful species with little desire to move; able to sit motionless for hours. Arboreal, but often seen on the ground.

IN BRIEF **Class:** *Reptiles* **Order:** *Scaled reptiles* **Suborder:** *Lizards* **Family:** *Iguanas* **Range:** *Southern Mexico to northeastern Colombia*

Helmeted Gecko

Geckonia chazaliae

Characteristics: TL 4 inches (10 cm), SVL 2½ inches (6 cm). Males stay smaller and slimmer and are identifiable by their hemipenes sacs (see page 26).

Terrarium type: 🌵
Level of difficulty: 1
Activity: ☀ 🌙
Habit: ⬇

Terrarium: Dry terrarium. Sand substrate, with lowest layer kept slightly moist. Cork walls that can be climbed are used now and then as a running surface. Provide hiding places under which the animals can stay in the daytime. Recommended terrarium size for housing an adult pair: 20 × 12 × 12 inches (50 × 30 × 30 cm). Add 15% to area for each additional female. Temperature 75–82.5°F (24–28°C), at night 61–68°F (16–20°C), basking islands 95°F (35°C). Atmospheric humidity 50–60%. Lighting: 10–12 hours.

Keeping/Care: Mist terrarium lightly every morning. Keep as a pair or as a group with only one male. Hibernation: 8–12 weeks at about 59°F (15°C).

Diet: Insects such as house crickets, cockroaches, field crickets, grasshoppers, and wax moth larvae.

Behavior: When threatened, these animals stand up on their hind legs and squeak with their mouths wide open.

IN BRIEF **Class:** *Reptiles* **Order:** *Scaled reptiles* **Suborder:** *Lizards* **Family:** *Geckos* **Range:** *Morocco, western Sahara, Mauritania to Senegal*

Henkel's Leaf-tailed Gecko

Uroplatus henkeli

Terrarium type: 🔼🔼
Level of difficulty: 1
Activity: ☀️
Habit: 🌳

Characteristics: TL 10½ inches (26 cm), SVL 6–6⅜ inches (15–16 cm). Males are yellow with large spots, females have dark speckling with a beige-gray body color.

Terrarium: Warm, humid woodland terrarium with smooth climbing branches, most of them vertically positioned. Keep moisture-retaining substrate slightly damp. Planting with smooth, stiff-leaved plants such as *Sansevieria* advisable. Provide hiding places. Recommended terrarium size for housing an adult pair: 36 × 36 × 48 inches (90 × 90 × 120 cm). Temperature 77–86°F (25–30°C), at night 68°F (20°C). Atmospheric humidity 85%. Lighting: 10–12 hours. UV radiation required.

Keeping/Care: Keep as a single animal or as a pair. Keep as a group with one male and several females *only* in very large terrariums. Hibernation: 6–8 weeks at 68–71.5°F (20–22°C), at night 61–64.5°F (16–18°C).

Diet: Field crickets, house crickets, and wax moths or their larvae. Calcium important for formation of hard-shelled eggs.

Behavior: When resting motionless on bark, they are hard to see because of their body color and excellent camouflage.

IN BRIEF **Class:** *Reptiles* **Order:** *Scaled reptiles* **Suborder:** *Lizards* **Family:** *Geckos* **Range:** *Madagascar, island Nosy Bé*

Hermann's Tortoise

Testudo hermanni

Characteristics: CL up to 10 inches (25 cm). Males stay smaller, with concave plastrons and longer, more powerful tails.

Terrarium type: 🌿 🌲
Level of difficulty: 1
Activity: ☀
Habit: ⛰

Terrarium: Recommended minimum size of dry terrarium or outdoor enclosure (length × width) for housing an adult pair: 80 × 40 inches (200 × 100 cm). Add 10% each for third and fourth specimens, then 20% more for each additional one. Temperature 68–95°F (20–35°C), at night 50–68°F (10–20°C), basking islands about 113°F (45°C). Atmospheric humidity 50–80%. Lighting: up to 12 hours. UV radiation required.

Keeping/Care: After compatibility test, keeping a group is possible. Outdoor housing advisable during summer months. Plants that give shade, sunny spots, and waterproof shelter are required. Replace water in drinking and bathing container daily. Hibernation: after slowly lowering temperature, 4–5 months at 41.5–46.5°F (5–8°C).

Diet: Dandelions, clover, leaf lettuce (not iceberg—it has almost no food value and can cause diarrhea, and vegetables. Calcium-containing supplements on a regular basis.

Behavior: Fond of digging. Quite lively for a tortoise.

IN BRIEF **Class:** *Reptiles* **Order:** *Tortoises and turtles*
Suborder: *Common-necked or straight-necked turtles*
Family: *Tortoises* **Range:** *In 2 subspecies, from the Balkans to southern France*

Hispaniolan Curly-tailed Lizard

Leiocephalus schreibersi

Also: Haitian curly-tailed lizard

Characteristics: TL 8⅞ inches (22 cm), SVL 4 inches (10 cm). Males are somewhat larger, with 2–3 pairs of larger postanal scales (see page 27), and with red and blue spots.

Terrarium type: 🌵
Level of difficulty: 1
Activity: ☼
Habit: ↓↓

Terrarium: Savannah terrarium. Sand substrate, 8 inches (20 cm) deep, kept slightly damp in several places. Provide hiding and climbing places. Water dish very important. Recommended terrarium size for housing an adult pair: 48 × 16 × 20 inches (120 × 40 × 50 cm). Temperature 81–90°F (27–32°C), at night 68°F (20°C), basking islands 95–104°F (35–40°C). Atmospheric humidity 50–60%. Very bright lighting: 12 hours. UV radiation required.

Keeping/Care: Keep as a pair. Hibernation: 2 months at 64.5–71.5°F (18–22°C) will stimulate reproduction.

Diet: House crickets, field crickets, flies, darkling beetle larvae, cockroaches, and small grasshoppers. Some individuals accept fruit and flowers.

Behavior: In the wild, the species inhabits open, desert-like sandy areas to undergrowth.

Similar needs: *Leiocephalus schreibersi nesomorus*

IN BRIEF **Class:** *Reptiles* **Order:** *Scaled reptiles* **Suborder:** *Lizards* **Family:** *Iguanas* **Range:** *Haiti and Dominican Republic*

Honduran Milk Snake

Lampropeltis triangulum hondurensis

Characteristics: TL up to 50 inches (125 cm). To ascertain sex, see page 15.

Terrarium: Woodland terrarium with climbing branches and hiding places. Mix soil with sand, peat, and leaves for substrate. Bathing pan, corresponding to snake's size, absolutely essential. Recommended terrarium size for housing an adult pair: 48 × 24 × 24 inches (120 × 60 × 60 cm). To keep a third specimen, add 20% to area. Air temperature 73.5–90°F (23–32°C), at night 64.5–81°F (18–27°C), water temperature 64.5–71.5°F (18–22°C), basking islands up to 95°F (35°C). Atmospheric humidity 60–80%. Lighting: 12 hours.

Keeping/Care: Keeping a pair or a group advisable only if they are the same size and are fed separately: danger of cannibalism. In winter, lower daytime and nighttime temperatures by 37.5°F (3°C); reduce lighting period to 6 hours.

Diet: Mice or rats of the appropriate size.

Behavior: In the daytime, hides in crevices or under stones and pieces of wood.

Terrarium type: ⌂⌂
Level of difficulty: 1
Activity: ☼
Habit: 💧

IN BRIEF   **Class:** *Reptiles* **Order:** *Scaled reptiles* **Suborder:** *Snakes* **Family:** *Colubrids* **Range:** *Eastern Honduras, Nicaragua, and northeastern Costa Rica*

Horned Tree Lizard

Acanthosaura crucigera

Also: horn-headed lizard

Characteristics: TL up to 15⅛ inches (38 cm), SVL 5⅝ inches (14 cm). Females less colorful, with less pronounced crosses on napes.

Terrarium type:
Level of difficulty: 3
Activity:
Habit:

Terrarium: Rainforest terrarium with ⅓ water portion. Furnish with climbing branches and rear wall suitable for climbing. Provide hiding places and retreats in the form of dense plantings. Recommended terrarium size for housing an adult pair: 48 × 24 × 48 inches (120 × 60 × 120 cm). Temperature 68–77°F (20–25°C), at night 59–68°F (15–20°C). Atmospheric humidity 70%, at night 90%. Lighting: 12 hours. UV radiation required.

Keeping/Care: Keep singly because even pregnant females are as aggressive as males. To breed, place animals in tank simultaneously, but then provide a visual barrier to permit hiding.

Diet: Grasshoppers, field crickets, wax moths, and moths, as well as worms and pinkie mice.

Behavior: Susceptible to stress. They avoid sunny and warm places. Without a water portion they will not thrive.

IN BRIEF **Class:** *Reptiles* **Order:** *Scaled reptiles*
Suborder: *Lizards* **Family:** *Agamas* **Range:** *Myanmar, Thailand, Laos, Cambodia, Vietnam to northern Malaysia*

Indian Ornamental Tarantula

Poecilotheria regalis

Characteristics: Body up to 2⅔ inches (7 cm). In the softened cast-off skin of the female's abdomen, semen sacs can be discerned.

Terrarium type: 🔼🔼
Level of difficulty: 2 !
Activity: ☀️ 🌙
Habit: 🌳

Terrarium: Modified woodland-type terrarium with climbing apparatus. Because the species inhabits hollow trees in the wild, provide a cork tube or piece of cork bark with an entry hole. Alternatively, hang up a birdhouse. Provide a shallow water dish or mist the terrarium daily. Depth of substrate: 1¼ inches (3 cm) is adequate. Recommended terrarium size for one adult: 10 × 12 × 16 inches (25 × 35 × 40 cm). Temperature 75–79°F (24–26°C), at night 68–71.5°F (20–22°C). Atmospheric humidity 70–80%. Lighting: 8–10 hours.

Keeping/Care: Keep male or female singly.

Diet: Depending on size, flies, wax moths, house crickets, cockroaches, and baby mammals.

Behavior: The species usually chooses flight over fight, but its bite can produce systemic effects. Be careful!

Similar needs: *Poecilotheria ornata, Poecilotheria fasciata*

IN BRIEF **Class:** *Arachnids* **Order:** *Spiders*
Suborder: *Tarantulas and relatives* **Family:** *Tarantulas*
Range: *Southwestern India and Sri Lanka* **Important:**
Results of a bite can range from dizziness lasting for days to chills and shivering.

Indian Star Tortoise

Geochelone elegans

Characteristics: CL up to 15¼ inches (38 cm). Males ⅓ smaller, with flatter, smoother carapaces, concave plastrons (see page 26), and longer tail.

Terrarium type: 🐢 🌲
Level of difficulty: 2
Activity: ☼
Habit: ↓↓

Terrarium: Woodland terrarium with soil substrate 5–8 inches (15–20 cm) deep, place for basking, dish for drinking and bathing water. Recommended area of terrarium or outdoor pen (length × width) for housing an adult pair: 120 × 60 inches (300 × 150 cm). Add 10% each for third and fourth specimens, then 20% for each additional one. Temperature 79–90°F (26–32°C), at night 64.5–71.5°F (18–22°C), basking islands up to 100°F (38°C). Atmospheric humidity varies widely, depending on origin of specimen. Lighting: 12–14 hours. UV radiation required.

Keeping/Care: Sensitive to drops in temperature. Wild-caught specimens often have trouble adapting to captivity. Susceptible to colds and parasites. Can be kept outdoors in summer. Places in sun and shade, as well as heated, waterproof shelter, required. After compatibility test, can be kept as a group.

Diet: Dandelions, clover, leaf lettuce, and vegetables. Fruit only once a week. Calcium preparations on a regular basis.

Behavior: Occurs in a wide variety of biotopes.

IN BRIEF **Class:** *Reptiles* **Order:** *Tortoises and turtles* **Suborder:** *Common-necked or straight-necked turtles* **Family:** *Tortoises* **Range:** *Southeastern Pakistan, India, and Sri Lanka*

Jeweled Lizard

Timon lepidus

Also: *Lacerta lepida*

Characteristics: TL 24–32 inches (60–80 cm), SVL 8⅜–11⅜ inches (21–29 cm). Males are bigger, with more massive heads and distinct femoral pores (see page 26). Females are smaller, no more than 20 inches (50 cm) long, and paler in color.

Terrarium: Dry terrarium with climbing walls and branches, hiding places, and a fairly large stone slab. Suitable substrate: sand or gravel, about 2 inches (5 cm) deep. Recommended terrarium size for housing an adult pair: 64 × 40 × 40 inches (160 × 100 × 100 cm). Temperature 73.5–82.5°F (23–28°C), at night 61–68°F (16–20°C), basking islands 95–113°F (35–45°C). Atmospheric humidity 60–70%. Lighting: 10–12 hours. UV radiation required.

Keeping/Care: Keep as a pair or as a group with only one male. Hibernation: 8 weeks at 50–64.5°F (10–18°C).

Diet: Grasshoppers, house crickets, field crickets, mealworms, and young mice. Fruit is also accepted.

Behavior: Predominantly ground-dwelling, but an excellent climber. Both males and females are territorial. The tail is easily detached if grabbed.

Terrarium type:

Level of difficulty: 1

Activity:

Habit:

IN BRIEF **Class:** *Reptiles* **Order:** *Scaled reptiles* **Suborder:** *Lizards* **Family:** *Wall lizards* **Range:** *Southern France to Portugal*

King Baboon Tarantula

Citharischius crawshayi

Terrarium type: 🌵
Level of difficulty: 3 !
Activity: ☼ ☽
Habit: ⤫

Characteristics: Body up to 4 inches (10 cm). Males smaller, with no tibial spurs (hook-like structures) and with somewhat longer hair.

Terrarium: Dry terrarium. Loamy soil at least 8 inches (20 cm) deep for burrowing, with lower layers kept slightly moist. Provide shallow water dish. Recommended terrarium size for one adult: 16 × 16 × 20 inches (40 × 40 × 50 cm). Temperature 77–86°F (25–30°C), at night 68–71.5°F (20–22°C). Atmospheric humidity 50–70%. Lighting: 8–10 hours.

Keeping/Care: Keep male or female singly. These are unpredictable and aggressive spiders that may also attack with lightning speed from their hiding places. Be very careful when working in the terrarium. Their venom is considered among the most toxic of tarantulas. Not for the beginner.

Diet: Depending on size, flies, wax moths, field crickets, grasshoppers, cockroaches, and baby rodents.

Behavior: Quite aggressive. In the wild they dig holes up to 6½ feet (2 m) deep, which they leave only at night to catch prey.

IN BRIEF **Class:** *Arachnids* **Order:** *Spiders*
Suborder: *Tarantulas and relatives* **Family:** *Tarantulas*
Range: *Uganda, Kenya, and Tanzania*

Knight Anole

Anolis equestris

Characteristics: TL 17–22 inches (45–55 cm), SVL 6–7 inches (15–18 cm). Males have colorful head patterns, larger throat pouches (dewlaps), and thickened tail bases.

Terrarium type:
Level of difficulty: 1
Activity:
Habit:

Terrarium: Moist woodland terrarium in well-lit location. Decorate with sturdy branches, placed horizontally and vertically. Plant with robust species. Substrate 4–6 inches (10–15 cm) deep. Recommended terrarium size for housing an adult pair 22 inches (55 cm) long: 44 × 44 × 60 inches (110 × 110 × 150 cm). Temperature 82.5–86°F (28–30°C), at night 68–77°F (20–25°C), basking islands 95°F (35°C). Atmospheric humidity 50–60%, at night 80–90%. Lighting: 12–14 hours. UV radiation required.

Keeping/Care: Keep as a pair or as a group with only one male. To simulate rainy season in fall, drop temperature by 43–46.5°F (6–8°C) for 8 weeks, reduce lighting by 4 hours, and slightly increase atmospheric humidity.

Diet: Large cockroaches, *Zophobas* larvae, grasshoppers, beetles, and young mice; rarely, fruit. Small drinking bowl important.

Behavior: In the wild, these animals leave their tree or bush only rarely, to pursue prey or lay eggs.

IN BRIEF **Class:** *Reptiles* **Order:** *Scaled reptiles*
Suborder: *Lizards* **Family:** *Iguanas* **Range:** *Cuba and Florida*

Land Hermit Crab

Coenobita spec.

Terrarium type: ◠
Level of difficulty: 1
Activity: ☽
Habit: ⏷⏷

Characteristics: TL 1⅛ inches (4 cm); soft body protected in empty snail shell.
Terrarium: Terrarium with two shallow dishes 4 inches (10 cm) across, one for fresh water, the other containing salt water to help maintain the crab's blood sodium level. Close-fitting cover to prevent escape. Substrate: fine gravel or river sand, in which the species likes to dig. Roots, bark, and stones for climbing. Keep one corner dry. Recommended terrarium size for one adult: 16 × 12 × 12 inches (40 × 30 × 30 cm). Air temperature 71.5–82.5°F (22–28°C), at night 63–68°F (17–20°C), water temperature in both dishes 77–82.5°F (25–28°C). Atmospheric humidity 70–90%. Lighting unnecessary if terrarium has a bright location.
Keeping/Care: Keep singly or in groups. Provide empty snail shells of different sizes as substitute housing. Prepare salt water from a sea salt mix for aquariums.
Diet: Lettuce, vegetables, fruit, pieces of meat and fish, fish food, and dead insects. Cuttlebone for calcium needs. Little food required. Place food in shallow containers to prevent fouling substrate.
Behavior: Undemanding terrarium occupants. When molting occurs, lost limbs are replaced.

IN BRIEF **Class:** *Crustaceans* **Order:** *Shrimps, crabs, and relatives* **Suborder:** *Crawling crustaceans* **Family:** *Land hermit crabs* **Range:** *Tropical coasts worldwide*

Large-clawed Scorpion

Scorpio maurus

Characteristics: TL, depending on subspecies, 2½–3¼ inches (6–8 cm). Males' bodies duller in color, pedipalps (claws) more compact.

Terrarium type: 🌵
Level of difficulty: 1 !
Activity: 🌙
Habit: ▨

Terrarium: Dry terrarium with sand-loam substrate, 4–8 inches (10–20 cm) deep. Keep bottom substrate layer slightly moist. Provide flat stones under which hollows can be dug. Supply shallow water dish. Recommended minimum area of terrarium (length × width) for housing one adult: 8 × 8 inches (20 × 20 cm). Temperature 86–95°F (30–35°C), at night 68–77°F (20–25°C). Atmospheric humidity 40–60%. Lighting: 8–10 hours.

Keeping/Care: Keep singly. If you ensure compatibility, 2–3 specimens also may be kept in one terrarium. The sting hurts only briefly, but is no more dangerous than a wasp sting.

Diet: House crickets, field crickets, pillbugs, grasshoppers, cockroaches, mealworms, and beetles.

Behavior: These animals, which are not quick to sting, are reluctant to leave their caves. The caves are constantly being expanded—in the wild, up to 3¼ feet (1 m) in length—and are only rarely abandoned.

IN BRIEF **Class:** *Arachnids* **Order:** *Scorpions*
Suborder: *Neoscorpionina* **Family:** *Scorpionidae*
Range: *Central to North Africa, Middle East to India*
Important: *Only slightly poisonous.*

Large-headed Anole

Anolis cybotes

Characteristics: TL 8 inches (20 cm), SVL 3¼ inches (8 cm). Females stay 15% smaller. Males have throat pouch (dewlap) and larger femoral pores (see page 26).

Terrarium type: 🌿
Level of difficulty: 1
Activity: ☀️
Habit: 🌳

Terrarium: Rainforest terrarium with dense plantings of *Ficus* species, bromeliads, ferns, and climbers that offer the animals shade, hiding places, and retreats. Furnish with climbing branches and roots. Substrate: mixture of sand and soil. Recommended terrarium size for housing an adult pair: 32 × 20 × 32 inches (80 × 50 × 80 cm). Temperature 75–79°F (24–26°C), at night 64.5–68°F (18–20°C), basking islands 95–104°F (35–40°C). Atmospheric humidity 50–60%. Lighting: 12–14 hours. UV radiation required.

Keeping/Care: Keep as a pair or as a group with one male. Hibernation: 2 months at room temperature.

Diet: House crickets, field crickets, and small grasshoppers. Now and then the animals will lick at mashed fruit or sweet fruits.

Behavior: Often roosts on trees pointing straight up, with outstretched head.

IN BRIEF **Class:** *Reptiles* **Order:** *Scaled reptiles* **Suborder:** *Lizards* **Family:** *Iguanas* **Range:** *Haiti, Dominican Republic, introduced in Florida*

Leopard Gecko

Eublepharis macularius

Also: Panther gecko, fat-tailed gecko

Characteristics: TL up to 10 inches (25 cm), SVL to 6 inches (15 cm). Males have bigger heads and thickened tail bases.

Terrarium type:	🌵
Level of difficulty:	1
Activity:	☀ 🌙
Habit:	⬇

Terrarium: Desert terrarium. Sand-loam mix, 4 inches (10 cm) deep, suitable for digging. Plant with succulents and drought-loving plants, ideally in pots. Provide hiding places. Recommended terrarium size for housing an adult pair: 32 × 24 × 12 inches (80 × 60 × 30 cm). For each additional female, add 15% to area. Temperature 82.5–86°F (28–30°C), at night 64.5–68°F (18–20°C). Atmospheric humidity 50–70%. Lighting: 10–12 hours.

Keeping/Care: Keep as a pair or as a group with only one male, as males do not get along together. Hibernation: 12–16 weeks at 59–64.5°F (15–18°C) required.

Diet: Insects such as house crickets, cockroaches, field crickets, and grasshoppers. Very young, still virtually hairless, rodents. Vitamin/mineral supplements are recommended.

Behavior: These animals, which inhabit steppe, sand, and rock deserts, quickly lose their shyness in a terrarium.

IN BRIEF **Class:** *Reptiles* **Order:** *Scaled reptiles* **Suborder:** *Lizards* **Family:** *Geckos* **Range:** *Iran, Afghanistan, Pakistan, and northwestern regions of India*

Leopard Tortoise

Geochelone pardalis

Characteristics: CL up to 28 inches (70 cm). *G. p. babcocki* females are larger.

Terrarium type: 🌵 🌳
Level of difficulty: 2
Activity: ☀️
Habit: ⬇️⬇️

Terrarium: Dry terrarium. Provide place to bask and water dish for drinking and bathing. Substrate: soil and sand, 2–4 inches (5–10 cm) deep. Recommended minimum area of terrarium or outdoor pen (length × width) for housing an adult pair: 224 × 112 inches (560 × 280 cm). For third and fourth specimens add 10%, then add 20% for each additional one. Temperature 82.5–95°F (28–35°C), at night 64.5–71.5°F (18–22°C), basking islands 104–113°F (40–45°C). Atmospheric humidity 50–60%. Lighting: 12–14 hours. UV radiation required.

Keeping/Care: After compatibility test, can be kept as a group. Can be kept outdoors in warm summer months. Shady and sunny places, as well as waterproof shelter, are required. Hibernation: 8 months at 68–77°F (20–25°C).

Diet: Dandelions, clover, romaine lettuce, and vegetables. Fruit no more than once a week. Calcium preparations on a regular basis.

Behavior: Susceptible to stress, so avoid frequent moves between outdoor pen and terrarium. Most offered for sale are small captive-raised individuals.

IN BRIEF   **Class:** *Reptiles* **Order:** *Turtles*
Suborder: *Common-necked or straight-necked turtles*
Family: *Tortoises* **Range:** *Sudan to Namibia*

Long-nosed Leopard Lizard

Gambelia wislizenii

Characteristics: TL up to 15¼ inches (38 cm), SVL 4⅜ inches (11 cm). Males smaller, slimmer, with enlarged postanal scales and femoral pores (see page 26).

Terrarium type: 🌵
Level of difficulty: 2
Activity: ☀
Habit: ⬇ ⬈

Terrarium: Dry terrarium with sandy substrate about 4–6 inches (10–15 cm) deep, suitable for digging. Hiding places under piles of stones. Recommended terrarium size for housing an adult pair: 64 × 20 × 24 inches (160 × 50 × 60 cm). Temperature 77–95°F (25–35°C), at night 64.5–71.5°F (18–22°C), basking islands 104°F (40°C). Lighting: 14 hours. UV radiation required.

Keeping/Care: Keep animals of like size as a pair or as a group with one male. Mist terrarium daily and provide small water dish, but avoid excessive humidity or dampness. Hibernation: 4–6 weeks at 50–59°F (10–15°C) will stimulate reproduction.

Diet: House crickets, field crickets, wax moth larvae, small lizards, and baby rodents; dandelions. In some cases, picky feeders.

Behavior: These lizards enjoy basking. They can walk upright on their hind limbs and use their tails to keep their balance. Shy; require long acclimation period.

IN BRIEF **Class:** *Reptiles* **Order:** *Scaled reptiles*
Suborder: *Lizards* **Family:** *Iguanas* **Range:** *Southwestern United States to northern Mexico*

Madagascar Giant Day Gecko

Phelsuma madagascariensis grandis

Terrarium type: 🏔
Level of difficulty: 1
Activity: ☼
Habit: 🌳

Characteristics: TL 11¼ inches (28 cm), SVL up to 6 inches (15 cm). From age of one year, males identifiable by easily visible preanofemoral pores (see page 27).

Terrarium: Humid woodland or rainforest terrarium with moist substrate. Furnish with smooth-leaved plants and smooth climbing branches. Provide hiding places. Recommended terrarium size for housing an adult pair: 36 × 36 × 48 inches (90 × 90 × 120 cm). Temperature 77–86°F (25–30°C), at night 64.5–73.5°F (18–23°C), basking islands 95–104°F (35–40°C). Atmospheric humidity 60–70%, at night 80–90%. Lighting: 10–12 hours. UV radiation required.

Keeping/Care: Keep as a pair. Don't separate compatible animals again. Be careful when touching them; the thin skin is easily torn, and scars are left after the injuries heal.

Diet: Field crickets, house crickets, grasshoppers, and cockroaches. Once a week, mashed fruit. Mineral supplements especially important for formation of hard-shelled eggs.

Behavior: In the wild, lives on trees, bushes, plants, and sometimes walls.

IN BRIEF **Class:** *Reptiles* **Order:** *Scaled reptiles*
Suborder: *Lizards* **Family:** *Geckos* **Range:** *Madagascar and offshore island Nosy Bohara*

Malayan Box Turtle

Cuora amboinensis

Characteristics: CL up to 8 inches (20 cm). Males stay smaller, with more oval carapace and broader, longer tail.

Terrarium type: ⌣
Level of difficulty: 1
Activity: ☼
Habit: ⬤

Terrarium: Aquatic terrarium with ⅔ water portion and good filtration. Water level no more than double the CL. Place something to climb on in the water portion, so that the turtles can get to the surface or onto the land. Substrate of land portion: mixture of sand and woodland soil. Recommended minimum area of a terrarium (length × width) for housing an adult pair: 48 × 24 inches (120 × 60 cm). Air temperature 81–86°F (27–30°C), at night 68–77°F (20–25°C), water temperature 77°F (25°C). Lighting: up to 12 hours. UV radiation required.

Keeping/Care: Sensitive to overly low temperatures, even over the short term. Keep as a pair; after testing for compatibility, may be kept as a group with several females.

Diet: Fish, earthworms, crustaceans, dry food for aquatic turtles, and occasionally fruit. Sometimes slightly fussy about its food.

Behavior: Withdraws inside its fully closed shell when alarmed.

IN BRIEF **Class:** *Reptiles* **Order:** *Tortoises and turtles*
Suborder: *Common-necked or straight-necked turtles*
Family: *Pond and box turtles* **Range:** *Southeast Asian area*

Malayan Crested Lizard

Gonocephalus grandis

Characteristics: TL 23 inches (58 cm), SVL 6¼ inches (16 cm). Males slightly larger, with dorsal crest and with body and tail more flattened laterally.

Terrarium type: 🌿
Level of difficulty: 2
Activity: ☀
Habit: 🌳

Terrarium: Rainforest terrarium with 50% water portion and water level of 4–6 inches (10–15 cm). Good water quality essential. Install climbing branches and rear wall suitable for climbing. Provide hiding places and retreats. Recommended terrarium size for housing an adult pair: 72 × 40 × 72 inches (180 × 100 × 180 cm). Temperature 68–77°F (20–25°C), at night 61–64.5°F (16–18°C), basking islands 86–95°F (30–35°C). Atmospheric humidity 85–100%. Lighting: 12 hours. UV radiation required.

Keeping/Care: Buy only captive-bred animals, as wild-caught specimens often bump on the panes until their mouths are bloody. Keep as a pair. To supply water, mist daily or provide waterfall.

Diet: Grasshoppers, cockroaches, field crickets, wax moths and their larvae, beetles, and baby mice.

Behavior: Lives in trees near bodies of water. Very good swimmer and diver. Fearful, with pronounced flight behavior.

IN BRIEF **Class:** *Reptiles* **Order:** *Scaled reptiles* **Suborder:** *Lizards* **Family:** *Agamas* **Range:** *Southern Thailand, Malaysia, northern Indonesian islands*

Malayan Painted Toad

Kaloula pulchra

Characteristics: SVL 2¾–3¼ inches (7–8 cm). Males have black vocal sac.

Terrarium: Aquatic terrarium with ⅓ water portion and water level of 2–4 inches (5–10 cm). Soil substrate, 8 inches (20 cm) deep, kept slightly damp. These toads love to dig, so put plants in flower pots. Alternatively, use peat slabs, which are easier to remove and clean. Provide hiding places under pieces of cork bark, flat stones, and roots. Recommended terrarium size for housing an adult pair: 32 × 14 × 16 inches (80 × 35 × 40 cm). Air temperature 71.5–79°F (22–26°C), at night 61–68°F (16–20°C), water temperature 77°F (25°C). Lighting: 10–12 hours.

Terrarium type: ◡
Level of difficulty: 1
Activity: ☼ ☽
Habit: ▭

Keeping/Care: Clean terrarium often because the species produces large amounts of feces. Easy to keep, apart from the noisy call of males in mating season, which can reach almost intolerable levels.

Diet: House crickets, field crickets, grasshoppers, wax moths, caterpillars, earthworms, and June bug larvae.

Behavior: In the wild, the species digs in backwards and spends the dry season in the ground. When threatened, it puffs up and extends its limbs.

IN BRIEF **Class:** *Amphibians* **Order:** *Frogs and toads* **Suborder:** *Modern or advanced frogs* **Family:** *Narrowmouth or microhylid frogs* **Range:** *India to China, Malaysia, and Indonesia*

Marbled Newt

Triturus marmoratus

Terrarium type: 〰️
Level of difficulty: 1
Activity: 🌙
Habit: ⬇️ 💧

Characteristics: TL, depending on subspecies, 4–6 inches (10–15 cm), SVL 1⅞–2¼ inches (4.5–5.5 cm). During mating period, males recognizable by high crest. Juveniles and females have a yellow-orange vertebral stripe on their backs.

Terrarium: Aquatic terrarium, land portion predominating, with hiding places under roots and stones. A drainage layer of expandable clay under the substrate prevents standing water. Alternatively, use a wet terrarium and transfer to an aquarium during reproductive period. Recommended terrarium size for an adult pair 6 inches (15 cm) long: 20 × 12 × 12 inches (50 × 30 × 30 cm). Add 25% to area for each additional specimen. Temperature 68–71.5°F (20–22°C), at night 61–64.5°F (16–18°C). Values can vary, depending on subspecies. Lighting: 10–12 hours.

Keeping/Care: These newts get along well together. To breed, hibernation period of 8 weeks at 41.5–46.5°F (5–8°C) is recommended.

Diet: Earthworms, *Tubifex*, water fleas, aquatic insects.

Behavior: Nocturnal, also diurnal during reproductive period in the water.

IN BRIEF **Class:** *Amphibians* **Order:** *Salamanders* **Suborder:** *Salamanders and their allies* **Family:** *Salamanders and newts* **Range:** *France and Spain*

Marbled Reed Frog

Hyperolius marmoratus

Characteristics: SVL up to 1¼ inches (3 cm). Females brilliantly colored. Males smaller, plain gray in color, with yellowish throat.

Terrarium type: 🌿
Level of difficulty: 2
Activity: ☀️ 🌙
Habit: 🌳

Terrarium: Rainforest terrarium with large water dish. Alternatively, aquatic terrarium with ¾ land portion and water level of 2–4 inches (5–10 cm). Create ramp to land area with peat slabs. Use moisture-retaining substrate, which may be covered with moss in some spots. Provide climbing branches. Furnish with green plants and climbers. Recommended terrarium size for up to 6 adults: 16 × 16 × 24 inches (40 × 40 × 60 cm). Air temperature 73.5–77°F (23–25°C), in places 82.5°F (28°C), at night 64.5–71.5°F (18–22°C), water temperature 77°F (25°C). Atmospheric humidity 50–70%. Lighting: 12–14 hours.

Keeping/Care: Males compete for calling places. They push each other and leap at each other, but engage in no serious fighting. As a breeding group, keep 2 males with 4 females.

Diet: Flies, wax moths, small house crickets, field crickets, or grasshoppers.

Behavior: In the daytime, they sleep on leaves or twigs with their limbs drawn close to their bodies (see photo, page 6).

IN BRIEF **Class:** *Amphibians* **Order:** *Frogs and toads* **Suborder:** *Modern or advanced frogs* **Family:** *African tree frogs* **Range:** *Eastern and southern Africa*

Marginated Tortoise

Testudo marginata

Characteristics: CL up to 14 inches (35 cm). Male has concave plastron (see page 26), markedly longer tail.

Terrarium: Dry terrarium, outdoor pen. Shade plants, sunny places, and shelter required. Provide water dish for drinking and bathing, and replace water daily. Recommended minimum size of terrarium or outdoor pen (length × width) for housing an adult pair: 112 × 56 inches (280 × 140 cm). For third and fourth specimens, add 10% each; for each additional specimen, increase area by 20%. Temperature 77–86°F (25–30°C), basking islands about 113°F (45°C). Atmospheric humidity 60–85%. Lighting: up to 12 hours. UV radiation required.

Keeping/Care: After compatibility test, may be kept as a group. Advisable to keep outdoors in summer. Hibernation: 5–7 months at 41.5–46.5°F (5–8°C).

Diet: Dandelions, clover, romaine lettuce, and vegetables. Give food supplements containing calcium on a regular basis.

Behavior: Prefers sunny places sheltered from the wind.

Terrarium type:
Level of difficulty: 1
Activity:
Habit:

IN BRIEF   Class: *Reptiles* **Order:** *Tortoises and turtles*
Suborder: *Common-necked or straight-necked turtles*
Family: *Tortoises* **Range:** *Greece, Aegean Islands, introduced on Sardinia and in Tuscany*

Martinique Pink-toe Tarantula

Avicularia versicolor

Characteristics: Body up to 2⅜ inches (6 cm). See page 9 for sexing.

Terrarium: Wet terrarium with branches and cork rear wall, as the species is fond of climbing. Leaf mold is a suitable substrate; always keep it damp, but never wet. Provide a water container. Recommended terrarium size for one adult: 12 × 12 × 16 inches (30 × 30 × 40 cm). Temperature 77–82.5°F (25–28°C), at night 68–73.5°F (20–23°C). Atmospheric humidity 70–85%. Lighting: 8–10 hours.

Keeping/Care: Keep male or female singly. The lamps should be attached outside the terrarium to prevent the spider from building its silk retreats on them. Don't keep the substrate too wet; the species is very sensitive to dampness.

Diet: Depending on size, flies, house crickets, and grasshoppers; baby mammals.

Behavior: Peaceful tree dweller, loves to move around. The females are aggressive only during mating.

Terrarium type:

Level of difficulty: 1

Activity:

Habit:

IN BRIEF **Class:** *Arachnids* **Order:** *Spiders*
Suborder: *Tarantulas and relatives* **Family:** *Tarantulas*
Range: *Martinique, Venezuela, and Guadeloupe*

Mediterranean Spur-thighed Tortoise

Testudo graeca

Characteristics: CL up to 12 inches (30 cm). Males smaller, with concave plastrons and bigger tails.

Terrarium type: 🌵 🌿
Level of difficulty: 3, 4
Activity: ☀️
Habit: 〰️

Terrarium: Recommended minimum size of a terrarium or outdoor pen (length × width) housing an adult pair: 96 × 48 inches (240 × 120 cm). For third or fourth specimen, add 10%; for each additional specimen, add 20% to area. Temperature 77–86°F (25–30°C), at night 63–71.5°F (17–22°C), basking islands about 113°F (45°C). Atmospheric humidity 70–90%. Lighting: up to 12 hours. UV radiation required.

Keeping/Care: European and Near Eastern form: difficulty level 3; African form, level 4. After compatibility test, may be kept as a group, Keep outdoors in summer. Requirements: places in sun and shade, as well as waterproof shelter. Replace water in drinking and bathing dish daily. Hibernation: 3–4 months at 41.5–50°F (5–10°C), after slow lowering of temperature.

Diet: Dandelions, clover, romaine lettuce, and vegetables. Mineral/vitamin supplement on a regular basis.

Behavior: Needs more warmth and is more susceptible to disease and stress than Hermann's tortoise (see page 149).

IN BRIEF **Class:** *Reptiles* **Order:** *Tortoises and turtles* **Suborder:** *Common-necked or straight-necked turtles* **Family:** *Tortoises* **Range:** *Southern Europe, Asia Minor, and northwestern Africa*

Mediterranean Yellow Scorpion

Buthus occitanus

Characteristics: TL about 3¼ inches (8 cm). Males ¼ smaller, with more pectinal teeth than females.

Terrarium type: 🌵
Level of difficulty: 2 !
Activity: ☽
Habit: 🔱

Terrarium: Dry terrarium. Substrate: sand and loamy soil. Furnish shallow water dish. Recommended terrarium size for one adult: 12 × 12 × 8 inches (30 × 30 × 20 cm). For European specimens, temperature 73.5°F (23°C), at night 64.5–68°F (18–20°C). atmospheric humidity 65%. For African specimens, temperature 95°F (35°C), at night 77°F (25°C), atmospheric humidity 50%. Lighting: 8–10 hours.

Keeping/Care: If keeping a pair, terrarium size and good feeding can sometimes prevent cannibalism. Hibernation: European specimens at 59°F (15°C), African specimens at 68°F (20°C).

Diet: House crickets, field crickets, grasshoppers, cockroaches, mealworms, beetles, and *Zophobas* larvae.

Behavior: These scorpions dig under flat stones to make retreats for themselves. Dangerous and agressive. Many Buthid scorpions have extemely potent venom, and stings from the African form of the species have cause numerous fatalities.

IN BRIEF **Class:** *Arachnids* **Order:** *Scorpions* **Suborder:** *Neoscorpionina* **Family:** Thick-tailed scorpions (Buthidae) **Range:** *Southern France, Spain, and Portugal; African population, North Africa to Middle East* **Important:** *The African specimens' venom can cause potentially fatal heart and circulatory problems!*

Mexican Fireleg Tarantula

Brachypelma boehmei

Also: *Brachypelma boehmi*

Characteristics: Body up to 2¾ inches (7 cm). See page 9 for sexing.

Terrarium type: 🌵
Level of difficulty: 2 !
Activity: ☀ ☾
Habit: ⬇

Terrarium: Dry terrarium, misted once a week. Soil substrate, about 2 inches (5 cm) deep. Provide caves of cork bark with diameter of about 6 inches (15 cm). Supply shallow water dish. Recommended terrarium size for one adult: 16 × 12 × 12 inches (40 × 30 × 30 cm). Temperature 81–90°F (27–32°C), at night 71.5–79°F (22–26°C). Atmospheric humidity 70%. Lighting: 8–10 hours.

Keeping/Care: Keep male or female singly. Be cautious when working on the terrarium, as these generally peaceful animals are very nervous and quick to defend themselves by flicking hairs (see page 20). A beautiful species.

Diet: Depending on size, flies, wax moths, field crickets, grasshoppers, cockroaches, and baby mammals.

Behavior: In the wild, digs tunnels more than 39 inches (1 m) long near the surface, where it retreats from the extreme heat after capturing prey.

IN BRIEF **Class:** *Arachnids* **Order:** *Spiders* **Suborder:** *Tarantulas and relatives* **Family:** *Tarantulas* **Range:** *Western Mexico* **Important:** *Scientifically described in 1994.*

Mexican Red-knee Tarantula

Brachypelma smithi

Also: Mexican red-rump tarantula

Characteristics: Body up to 2⅞ inches (7 cm). See page 9 for sexing.

Terrarium: Dry terrarium with substrate 2–4 inches (5–10 cm) deep: mixture of soil or loamy earth with sand. Provide caves of cork bark with a diameter of about 6 inches (15 cm). Supply shallow water dish. Recommended terrarium size for one adult: 16 × 12 × 12 inches (40 × 30 × 30 cm). Temperature 77–82.5°F (25–28°C), at night 68–73.5°F (20–23°C). Atmospheric humidity 70–80%. Lighting: 8–10 hours.

Keeping/Care: Keep male or female singly. Be sure to stay within temperature and atmospheric humidity ranges.

Diet: Depending on size, flies, house crickets, and grasshoppers, as well as baby rodents and small lizards. Some individuals are very choosy and refuse certain types of food.

Behavior: The species builds tubular webs. These spiders are not very active. They defend themselves by flicking hairs (see page 20). Do not let hairs get in your eyes.

Terrarium type:

Level of difficulty: 2 !

Activity:

Habit:

IN BRIEF **Class:** *Arachnids* **Order:** *Spiders* **Suborder:** *Tarantulas and relatives* **Family:** *Tarantulas* **Range:** *Mexico*

Mexican Red-legged Tarantula

Brachypelma emilia

Characteristics: Body up to 2½ inches (6 cm) long. Males darker than females. See page 9 for additional sexing information.

Terrarium type: 🌵
Level of difficulty: 1 !
Activity: ☀ ☾
Habit: ⚊

Terrarium: Dry terrarium. Soil substrate about 2–4 inches (5–10 cm) deep. Provide cork bark cave with diameter of about 6 inches (15 cm) and shallow water dish. Recommended terrarium size for one adult: 16 × 12 × 12 inches (40 × 30 × 30 cm). Temperature 75–79°F (24–26°C), at night 68°F (20°C). Atmospheric humidity 60–70%. Lighting: 8–10 hours.

Keeping/Care: Keep male or female singly. Be cautious when working on the terrarium. Even small provocations cause the species to defend itself by flicking the fine hairs from its abdomen and hind legs. While the hairs cause prolonged itching on the face and hands, if inhaled they can result in difficulty in breathing. Do not get them in your eyes.

Diet: Depending on size, flies, wax moths, house crickets, field crickets, cockroaches, and baby rodents.

Behavior: Seeks out cavities under stones or pieces of cork bark as hiding places. The species is often aggressive in its behavior. A popular species.

IN BRIEF **Class:** *Arachnids* **Order:** *Spiders* **Suborder:** *Tarantulas and relatives* **Family:** *Tarantulas* **Range:** *Mexico to Panama*

Mexican Redrump Tarantula

Brachypelma vegans

Characteristics: Body up to 3¼ inches (8 cm). See page 9 for sexing information.

Terrarium type: 🔺🔺
Level of difficulty: 1 !
Activity: 😷 🌙
Habit: 🔽

Terrarium: Humid forest terrarium with 4-inch (10-cm) deep substrate, slightly damp. Provide caves in the form of cork bark with a diameter of about 6 inches (15 cm). Supply shallow water dish. Recommended terrarium size for one adult: 16 × 12 × 12 inches (40 × 30 × 30 cm). Temperature 77–81°F (25–27°C), at night 64.5–68°F (18–20°C). Atmospheric humidity 70–80%. Lighting: 8–10 hours.

Keeping/Care: Keep male or female singly. Though the majority of captive animals are peaceful and patient, there are reports of some aggressive individuals. A popular and hardy beginner's tarantula species.

Diet: Depending on size, flies, house crickets, grasshoppers, small lizards, and baby rodents.

Behavior: Digs tubes up to 20 inches (50 cm) deep to live in.

IN BRIEF **Class:** *Arachnids* **Order:** *Spiders* **Suborders:** *Tarantulas and relatives* **Family:** *Tarantulas* **Range:** *Savannahs and rainforest areas, Mexico to Colombia*

Mississippi Map Turtle

Graptemys pseudogeographica kohni

Terrarium type: 〰
Level of difficulty: 2
Activity: ☼
Habit: ◇

Characteristics: CL up to 10½ inches (26 cm). Males stay smaller and have longer claws on forelimbs and much longer tails.

Terrarium: Aquatic terrarium with ⅔ water portion. The water level should be deep enough for swimming and diving. Recommended minimum size of a terrarium (length × width) for housing an adult pair: 56 × 28 inches (140 × 70 cm). Air temperature 79–81°F (26–27°C), at night 68–70°F (20–21°C), water temperature 73.5–79°F (23–26°C), basking islands about 95°F (35°C). Lighting: up to 16 hours. UV radiation required.

Keeping/Care: Sensitive to poor water quality. Keep as a pair or, after compatibility test, as a group with several females. Hibernation: 6–8 weeks at 59–63°F (15–17°C).

Diet: Fish, earthworms, crustaceans, small aquatic snails, and pieces of fish. Also gelatin-based foods and dry foods for aquatic turtles. Increase proportion of plant foods with increasing age.

Behavior: Relatively shy. In the wild, these turtles prefer quiet bodies of water with dense vegetation.

IN BRIEF **Class:** *Reptiles* **Order:** *Scaled reptiles* **Suborder:** *Common-necked or straight-necked turtles* **Family:** *Pond and box turtles* **Range:** *Southwestern United States*

Mojave Collared Lizard

Crotaphytus insularis bicinctores

Terrarium type: 🌵
Level of difficulty: 1
Activity: ☀
Habit:

Characteristics: TL 14 inches (35 cm), SVL 4 inches (10 cm). Males have more brilliant colors, distinct femoral pores, and large postanal scales (see page 26).

Terrarium: Steppe terrarium with sand-loam substrate 4 inches (10 cm) deep. Include drought-loving plants in flower pots or artificial plants. Provide stable pile of stones and large roots as hiding places. Small water pan. Recommended terrarium size for housing an adult pair: 48 × 20 × 28 inches (120 × 50 × 70 cm). Temperature 82.5–95°F (28–35°C), at night 64.5–71.5°F (18–22°C), basking islands 113°F (45°C). Atmospheric humidity 50–60%. Lighting: 14 hours. UV radiation required.

Keeping/Care: Keep as a single animal or as a pair. Can be territorial and cannibalistic. In winter, keep at 50–53.5°F (10–12°C) for 8–12 weeks. Shy; bites hard when you try to take hold of it.

Diet: Field crickets, grasshoppers, cockroaches, smaller lizards, and baby rodents. Occasionally flowers, leaves, fruit. Vitamin/mineral supplementation.

Behavior: Lively species that can walk upright on its hind legs and uses its tail for stability. Will not feed if kept too cool.

IN BRIEF **Class:** *Reptiles* **Order:** *Scaled reptiles*
Suborder: *Lizards* **Family:** *Iguanas* **Range:** *Southern United States to northwestern Mexico*

Mombasa Golden Starburst Tarantula

Pterinochilus murinus

Also: *Pterinochilus sp. usambara,*
Pterinochilus mammilatus

Terrarium type: 🌿
Level of difficulty: 3 !
Activity: ☼ ☽
Habit: 🔅 🔆

Characteristics: Body up to 2½ inches (6 cm). See page 9 for sexing. Males stay smaller.

Terrarium: Wet terrarium with substrate of sand/peat mixture, 2–4 inches (5–10 cm) deep. Place climbing branches and bent cork pieces or tubes in vertical position. Supply water container. Recommended terrarium size for one adult: 12 × 12 × 16 inches (30 × 30 × 40 cm). Temperature 77–86°F (25–30°C), at night 68–73.5°F (20–23°C). Atmospheric humidity 70–80%. Lighting: 8–10 hours.

Keeping/Care: Keep male or female singly, except to attempt mating. More easily bred than most tarantulas.

Diet: Depending on size, flies, house crickets, grasshoppers, baby rodents.

Behavior: Fast-moving species that likes to dig and busily weaves webs. Mainly terrestrial. These spiders are quick to attack and bite without warning. Their bites are particularly painful.

IN BRIEF **Class:** *Arachnids* **Order:** *Spiders* **Suborder:** *Tarantulas and relatives* **Family:** *Tarantulas* **Range:** *Kenya, Mozambique, Tanzania* **Important:** *Poisonous and quick. Spider bites on the hand can result in stiffness of the fingers for an extended period of time.*

Mountain Horned Dragon

Acanthosaura capra

Also: Horned mountain dragon, mountain horned lizard

Terrarium type: 🌿
Level of difficulty: 1
Activity: ☀️
Habit: ❄️ 🌳

Characteristics: TL up to 12¼ inches (32 cm), SVL 4¾ inches (12 cm). Females more massive, males have thickened tail bases.

Terrarium: Rainforest terrarium with ¼ water portion. Furnish with climbing branches and rear wall that can be climbed. Provide places to hide and retreat in the form of dense plantings. Substrate: soil and peat. Recommended terrarium size for housing an adult pair: 40 × 20 × 40 inches (100 × 50 × 100 cm). Temperature 73.5–77°F (23–25°C), at night 68°F (20°C). Atmospheric humidity 70%, at night 90%. Lighting: 12 hours. UV radiation required.

Keeping/Care: If overfed, these animals quickly become overweight. To supply water, mist daily or set up waterfall.

Diet: House crickets, grasshoppers, field crickets, flies, moths, earthworms, *Zophobas* larvae, wax moths and their larvae, caterpillars, and baby rodents.

Behavior: Peaceful animals that are excellent climbers and jumpers. They avoid direct heat or light (keep in mind when setting up terrarium!).

IN BRIEF **Class:** *Reptiles* **Order:** *Scaled reptiles*
Suborder: *Lizards* **Family:** *Agamas* **Range:** *Laos, Cambodia, and Vietnam*

Mourning Gecko

Lepidodactylus lugubris

Terrarium type: 🏔🏔
Level of difficulty: 1
Activity: ☀ ☾
Habit: 🌳

Characteristics: TL 3¼–4 inches (8–10 cm), SVL 1½–1⅞ inches (3.5–4.5 cm).
Terrarium: Woodland terrarium with cork rear wall that can be climbed and climbing branches. Substrate: sand or sandy soil, which may be sprinkled with pieces of bark and cork. Recommended terrarium size for 3–4 adults: 12 × 12 × 20 inches (30 × 30 × 50 cm). Temperature 79–82.5°F (26–28°C), at night 68–71.5°F (20–22°C). Atmospheric humidity 60–70%. Lighting: 10 hours.
Keeping/Care: Keep as a pair or as a group. Overall, the species is very peaceable; females form territories and hierarchies and are more aggressive than males, so don't overcrowd. Rear young geckos hatched in the terrarium in a separate terrarium of their own, and feed them small insects.
Diet: Small to medium-sized field crickets, house crickets, grasshoppers, wax moths and their larvae, flies, and pillbugs. Also fond of licking sweet fruit and honey. Supply mineral supplement.
Behavior: Predominantly asexual reproduction without males (virgin birth, parthenogenesis).

IN BRIEF **Class:** *Reptiles* **Order:** *Scaled reptiles*
Suborder: *Lizards* **Family:** *Geckos* **Range:** *Southeast Asia, Pacific islands to western America*

Niger Spiny-tailed Lizard

Uromastyx geyri

Characteristics: TL 15¼ inches (38 cm), SVL 8⅜ inches (21 cm). Males have yellowish, pinhead-sized femoral pores (see page 26). Red and yellow color varieties exist.

Terrarium type: 🌵
Level of difficulty: 2
Activity: ☀
Habit: 🔆 ⬓

Terrarium: Savannah terrarium. Mix of sand and loam 6–12 inches (15–30 cm) deep. Provide hiding places under stone and cork slabs. Recommended terrarium size for housing an adult pair: about 48 × 40 × 30 inches (120 × 100 × 75 cm). Temperature 90–95°F (32–35°C), at night 64.5–68°F (18–20°C), basking islands 113°F (45°C). Atmospheric humidity 40–60%. Lighting: very high light intensity, up to 14 hours. UV radiation required.

Keeping/Care: Advisable to keep as a pair or trio. High temperatures necessary for digestive function. Hibernation: 4 months at 53.5–64.5°F (12–18°C).

Diet Omnivorous. Feed moderately with chopped collard greens, escarole, romaine lettuce, yellow squash, sunflower seeds, grains, corn, rice, millet, crickets in small quantities. Gut-load insects before feeding or use vitamin/mineral supplements.

Behavior: Fond of digging. Like all other *Uromastyx* species, changes its color to regulate body temperature.

IN BRIEF **Class:** *Reptiles* **Order:** *Scaled reptiles*
Suborder: *Lizards* **Family:** *Agamas* **Range:** *Southern Algeria to northern Mali. Wild-caught specimens often adapt poorly to captive conditions.*

Northern Blue-tongued Skink

Tiliqua scincoides intermedia

Also: Common bluetongue

Characteristics: TL 20 inches (50 cm), SVL 10 inches (25 cm). Males usually have thicker tail base and wider heads.

Terrarium type: 🌵
Level of difficulty: 1
Activity: ☼
Habit: ⬐

Terrarium: Steppe terrarium with sand or fine gravel substrate, 4–6 inches (10–15 cm) deep. Plant with robust plants, ideally in pots. Provide hiding places on the ground in the form of flat stone slabs and cork tubes. Container of drinking water necessary. Recommended terrarium size for housing an adult pair: 60 × 40 × 30 inches (150 × 100 × 75 cm). Temperature 82.5–90°F (28–32°C), at night 64.5–68°F (18–20°C), basking islands up to 104°F (40°C), will be in frequent use. Atmospheric humidity 30–40%. Lighting: 12–14 hours. UV radiation required.

Keeping/Care: Keep as a pair or as a group with one male. Hibernation: 8–12 weeks at 68–77°F (20–25°C).

Diet: Omnivorous. Vegetables, green plants, and fruit, as well as grasshoppers, field crickets, house crickets, snails, and earthworms. The species has a tendency to become overweight.

Behavior: These animals grow quite tame in a terrarium. If threatened, they open their mouths wide and hiss, showing their blue tongues.

IN BRIEF **Class:** *Reptiles* **Order:** *Scaled reptiles*
Suborder: *Lizards* **Family:** *Skinks* **Range:** *Northeastern to southern Australia*

Northern Curly-tailed Lizard

Leiocephalus carinatus

Characteristics: TL 10⅛ inches (26 cm), SVL 4–5³⁄₁₆ inches (10–13 cm). Males have black banding from throat to neck area during mating season.

Terrarium type:	🌵
Level of difficulty:	1
Activity:	☼
Habit:	⤼⤼

Terrarium: Savannah terrarium. Sand substrate 8 inches (20 cm) deep, kept slightly damp in some spots. Mainly terrestrial, but provide places to climb and hide. Recommended terrarium size for housing an adult pair: 60 × 20 × 32 inches (150 × 50 × 80 cm). Temperature 77–86°F (25–30°C), at night 64.5–68°F (18–20°C), basking islands 95–104°F (35–40°C). Atmospheric humidity 50–60%. Very bright lighting: 12 hours. UV radiation required.

Keeping/Care: Keep as a pair, in large terrariums also with 2 females. For 8 weeks at the turn of the year, reduce lighting period and lower temperature to 64.5–68°F (18–20°C).

Diet: Beetles, darkling beetle larvae, cockroaches, house crickets, field crickets, small grasshoppers, meadow plankton. These lizards also accept flowers, buds, and smaller fruits. Supply dish of drinking water.

Behavior: Though ground-dwelling, the species climbs onto trees and rocks when in danger. In threatening situations and in combat, it curls its tail over its back.

IN BRIEF **Class:** *Reptiles* **Order:** *Scaled reptiles*
Suborder: *Lizards* **Family:** *Iguanas* **Range:** *From Cuba to Florida*

Orange-eyed Crocodile Skink

Tribolonotus gracilis

Also: Red-eyed armored skink, red-eyed casque-headed skink

Terrarium type:	🌿
Level of difficulty:	2
Activity:	☀️ 🌙
Habit:	🔅

Characteristics: TL about 8 inches (20 cm), SVL up to 4 inches (10 cm). Males identifiable after several months by larger, whitish pores on fourth and fifth toes of hind legs.

Terrarium: Rainforest terrarium with moisture-retaining substrate such as peat/sphagnum mixture, 1¼–2 inches (3–5 cm) deep. Provide hiding places under pieces of bark, stone slabs, and roots. A waterfall will be eagerly accepted as a place to climb and will make the skink happier. Recommended terrarium size for housing an adult pair: 32 × 16 × 12 inches (80 × 40 × 30 cm). Temperature 77–86°F (25–30°C), at night 64.5–71.5°F (18–22°C), basking islands about 95°F (35°C). Atmospheric humidity 80–90%. Lighting: 10–12 hours.

Keeping/Care: Keep as a pair. Males very aggressive toward each other. Several females cannot be housed together over the long run, even in large terrariums, as they will kill each other.

Diet: Earthworms, caterpillars, house crickets, and snails.

Behavior: After acclimation period, also visible during the day. Loud territorial calls. Seldom digs and climbs.

IN BRIEF **Class:** *Reptiles* **Order:** *Scaled reptiles* **Suborder:** *Lizards* **Family:** *Skinks* **Range:** *New Guinea, Solomon Islands, and New Caledonia*

Oriental Fire-bellied Toad

Bombina orientalis

Characteristics: SVL up to 2½ inches (6 cm). Males are clearly smaller, have nuptial pads (see page 26) on the inner surface of the forelegs during mating season.

Terrarium type: ⌒
Level of difficulty: 1
Activity: ☼ ⋈ ☾
Habit: ⋎⋎ ◯

Terrarium: Aquatic terrarium with large water portion 2–4 inches (5–10 cm) deep and banks that flatten out to give easy access. Provide hiding places. Terrarium size for up to 3 adult animals: 24 × 16 × 16 inches (60 × 40 × 40 cm); for housing 6–8 adults, 36 × 16 × 16 inches (90 × 40 × 40 cm) is adequate. Temperature 68–77°F (20–25°C), at night 64.5–68°F (18–20°C), water temperature 71.5–75°F (22–24°C). Atmospheric humidity 60–80%. Lighting: 10–12 hours. Spotlight for basking.

Keeping/Care: Because of their voracious appetites and possessiveness toward food, don't keep too many animals together. Distribute the food in several spots. For 8–12 weeks in winter, lower the temperature to 59–64.5°F (15–18°C) and the water level to 2 inches (5 cm). Do not keep too warm.

Diet: Flies, field crickets, worms, and slugs.

Behavior: In the wild, they stay near stretches of standing water during the reproductive period; at other times they prefer somewhat more rapidly flowing streams. Fond of basking.

IN BRIEF   Class: *Amphibians* **Order:** *Frogs and toads*
Suborder: *Ancient or primitive frogs* **Family:** *Fire-bellied toads*
Range: *Northeastern China to Korea*

Ornate Spiny-tailed Agama

Uromastyx ocellata

Characteristics: TL 12⅝ inches (32 cm), SVL 6¾ inches (17 cm). Males more brilliantly colored, with more prominent femoral pores (see page 26).

Terrarium type: 🌵
Level of difficulty: 2
Activity: ☀️
Habit: ⬓

Terrarium: Savannah terrarium with substrate 6–12 inches (15–30 cm) deep, suitable for digging. Stable piles of stones for climbing, with cavities beneath. Recommended terrarium size for housing an adult pair: about 40 × 28 × 20 inches (100 × 70 × 50 cm). Mist terrarium 2–3 times each week. Temperature 90–95°F (32–35°C), at night 64.5–68°F (18–20°C), basking islands 104–113°F (40–45°C). Atmospheric humidity 50–60%. Lighting: up to 14 hours. UV radiation required.

Keeping/Care: A pair is recommended. High temperatures are important for digestive system; feed moderately. Hibernation: 3 months at 50–59°F (10–15°C), but not necessary if kept warm enough.

Diet: Chopped greens and vegetables, sunflower seeds, grain, corn, rice, millet, and, occasionally, insects, baby mice, and mineral/vitamin supplements.

Behavior: Fond of digging, good climbers. They excrete excess salts through their nasal glands.

IN BRIEF **Class:** *Reptiles* **Order:** *Scaled reptiles* **Suborder:** *Lizards* **Family:** *Agamas* **Range:** *With 4 subspecies, from Egypt to the Arabian peninsula as well as Somalia and Eritrea*

Panther Chameleon

Furcifer pardalis

Characteristics: TL 20 inches (50 cm), SVL 8–10 inches (20–25 cm). Males identifiable quite early in life by hemipenal bulge (see page 26).

Terrarium type: 🌿
Level of difficulty: 2
Activity: ☀
Habit: 🌳

Terrarium: Rainforest terrarium with lots of horizontal, not overly thick climbing branches. Plantings recommended. Recommended terrarium size for housing an adult: 50 × 30 × 80 inches (125 × 75 × 200 cm). Temperature 71.5–82.5°F (22–28°C), at night 68–71.5°F (20–22°C), basking islands 95°F (35°C). Atmospheric humidity 70–100%. Up to 14 hours of very bright lighting. UV radiation required.

Keeping/Care: Territorial, so keep singly; only put pairs together for breeding and separate after mating has occurred. Mist terrarium daily. A specimen's refusal to eat may be due to lack of water. A drip system is recommended. Chameleons resent being disturbed. Do not unnecessarily handle.

Diet: Field crickets, house crickets, cockroaches, grasshoppers, and baby rodents. Gut-load insects before feeding.

Behavior: Less pronounced need for fresh air than other species and thus easier to keep.

IN BRIEF **Class:** *Reptiles* **Order:** *Scaled reptiles* **Suborder:** *Lizards* **Family:** *Chameleons* **Range:** *Madagascar, also introduced on Mauritius and Réunion* **Important:** *A large, strikingly beautiful species.*

Peacock Day Gecko

Phelsuma quadriocellata

Characteristics: TL, depending on subspecies, 3¼–5¼ inches (8–13 cm); SVL 1½–2⅝ inches (3.5–6.5 cm). Adult males identifiable by preanofemoral pores (see page 27).

Terrarium type: 🏞
Level of difficulty: 1
Activity: ☼
Habit: 🌳

Terrarium: Moist woodland terrarium with moist substrate. Provide hiding places and smooth branches, such as bamboo, for climbing. Smooth-leaved plants are ideal. Recommended terrarium size for housing an adult pair 5¼ inches (13 cm) long: 32 × 32 × 40 inches (80 × 80 × 100 cm). Temperature 77–82.5°F (25–28°C), at night 64.5–68°F (18–20°C), basking islands 86–91.5°F (30–33°C). Atmospheric humidity 60–80%, at night over 90%. Values can differ, depending on subspecies. Lighting: 10–12 hours. UV radiation required.

Keeping/Care: Keep as a pair. Do not separate compatible animals again. Depending on subpecies, very low hibernation temperature required.

Diet: Field crickets, house crickets, small grasshoppers, and cockroaches. Once a week, mashed fruit. Calcium supplements.

Behavior: In the wild, likes to live on banana plants.

IN BRIEF **Class:** *Reptiles* **Order:** *Scaled reptiles*
Suborder: *Lizards* **Family:** *Geckos* **Range:** *Eastern coast of Madagascar, especially in the region of Andasibe*

Pegu Forest Gecko

Cyrtodactylus peguensis

Also: Leopard forest gecko

Characteristics: TL 6 inches (15 cm), SVL 2¾ inches (7 cm). Males and females make whistling sounds, and the females also make croaking defensive noises.

Terrarium type:	🌿
Level of difficulty:	1
Activity:	☀️ 🌙
Habit:	〰️ 🌳

Terrarium: Rainforest terrarium with cork wall suitable for climbing and climbing branches. Substrate: mixture of peat, soil, and sand, ⅞–1¼ inches (2–3 cm) deep, covered with leaves. Provide cork tubes as hiding places. Plant climbers and green plants. Recommended terrarium size for housing an adult pair: 16 × 16 × 24 inches (40 × 40 × 60 cm). Add 15% to area for each additional female. Temperature 75–81°F (24–27°C), at night 68–71.5°F (20–22°C). Atmospheric humidity 70–80%. Lighting: 10 hours.

Keeping/Care: Keep as a pair or as a group with one male. Sensitive to dry air and high temperatures.

Diet: Small to medium-sized field crickets, house crickets, grasshoppers, wax moths and their larvae, and mineral supplements.

Behavior: Lives on the ground and in trees in rainforests near bodies of water.

IN BRIEF **Class:** *Reptiles* **Order:** *Scaled reptiles* **Suborder:** *Lizards* **Family:** *Geckos* **Range:** *Myanmar, Thailand, and Malaysia*

Phantasmal Poison Frog

Epipedobates tricolor

Also: Phantasmal poison-arrow frog
Characteristics: SVL 1¼ inches (3 cm).
The males are smaller and less rounded
than the females.

Terrarium type:
Level of difficulty: 1
Activity:
Habit:

Terrarium: Rainforest terrarium with 20% water portion
or large water dish. Substrate: peat slabs or forest soil. Provide
coconut shells as places to hide or lay eggs. Recommended
terrarium size for housing an adult pair: 16 × 16 × 20 inches
(40 × 40 × 50 cm). Double the size for up to 6 specimens.
Temperature 71.5–77°F (22–25°C), at night 68°F (20°C), water
temperature 75°F (24°C). Atmospheric humidity 80–90%, at
night 90–100%. Lighting: 12–14 hours.

Keeping/Care: Keep as a pair or a group.

Diet: Fruit flies, houseflies, aphids, small meadow plankton, and
small wax moths and their larvae. Regular doses of vitamins and
calcium.

Behavior: The females are very peaceful, but the males are territorial. These animals are susceptible to stress, easily frightened,
and amazingly loud for their tiny size.

IN BRIEF   **Class:** *Amphibians* **Order:** *Frogs and toads*
Suborder: *Modern or advanced frogs* **Family:** *Poison-dart*
frogs **Range:** *Wet forests from southwestern Ecuador to Peru*

Plains Garter Snake

Thamnophis radix

Terrarium type:
Level of difficulty: 1
Activity:
Habit:

Characteristics: TL up to 40 inches (100 cm). Females usually longer and more massive. To ascertain sex, see page 15.

Terrarium: Savannah terrarium with large bathing pan. Provide roots, piles of stones, and cork bark as hiding places, and dry basking places. Recommended terrarium size for housing an adult pair: 50 × 30 × 20 inches (125 × 75 × 50 cm). For each additional specimen, add 20% to area. Air temperature 75–79°F (24–26°C), at night 61–68°F (16–20°C), water at room temperature, basking islands 86°F (30°C). Values may be higher or lower, depending on geographic origin. Atmospheric humidity 50–60%. Lighting: 12 hours, partly UV.

Keeping/Care: May be kept as a group, since these snakes get along well together. Replace water and substrate regularly, as the stool is watery. Hibernation: 8 weeks at 50–59°F (10–15°C), animals of northern origin at 41.5–50°F (5–10°C).

Diet: Earthworms, fish, frogs, small rodents.

Behavior: Though lively in the terrarium, usually relatively shy. Fond of basking.

IN BRIEF **Class:** *Reptiles* **Order:** *Scaled reptiles* **Suborder:** *Snakes* **Family:** *Colubrids* **Range:** *Extreme south central Canada south through U.S. plains states*

Praying Mantid

Sphodromantis spec.

Characteristics: TL 3¼ inches (8 cm).
Terrarium: Woodland terrarium with dense plantings. Upward-angled climbing branches make good places to sit on or hang from. Recommended terrarium size for housing a single specimen: 8 × 8 × 10 inches (20 × 20 × 25 cm); for housing a pair: 12 × 12 × 10 inches (30 × 30 × 25 cm). Temperature 77–86°F (25–30°C), at night 64.5–68°F (18–20°C), basking islands 95°F (35°C). Atmospheric humidity 60–80%. Lighting: 10–12 hours.

Keeping/Care: These mantid tend to have molting problems and are sensitive to cigarette smoke. Make sure the terrarium is well ventilated; ideally, use wire mesh as a cover. Cannibalistic. Advisable to put pair together only for breeding. Males are often eaten by the females after mating (so-called sexual cannibalism).
Diet: Field crickets, house crickets, grasshoppers, cockroaches, flies, wax moth larvae, and mealworms.
Behavior: While the lyphs also spend time in the grass, adults are found on bushes and trees. They wait unmoving for their prey and seize it in a lightning-fast pounce.

Terrarium type: 🔲
Level of difficulty: 2
Activity: ☀
Habit: 🌳

IN BRIEF **Class:** *Insects* **Order:** *Mantids and praying mantids* **Family:** *Mantids* **Range:** *West Africa to East Africa*

Prehensile-tailed Skink

Corucia zebrata

Also: Solomon Islands skink, monkey-tailed skink

Terrarium type: 🌿
Level of difficulty: 2
Activity: 🌙
Habit: 🌳

Characteristics: TL 28 inches (70 cm), SVL 12 inches (30 cm). Very hard to sex. Sex can be reliably determined only through endoscopy, performed by a veterinarian.

Terrarium: Rainforest terrarium with lots of hiding places and hollow trees. Climbing branches 50% thicker than the animals' bodies. Recommended terrarium size for housing an adult pair: 48 × 36 × 60 inches (120 × 90 × 150 cm). Add 15% to area for each additional female. Temperature 79–86°F (26–30°C), at night 75°F (24°C), basking islands 104°F (40°C). Atmospheric humidity 75%. Lighting: 14 hours.

Keeping/Care: Keep as a pair or in groups with one male. If atmospheric humidity is too low, molting problems or even loss of the toes can result.

Diet: Chopped greens and vegetables such as zucchini and yellow squash. Mineral supplementation important.

Behavior: Arboreal species, spends the day sleeping in hollow trees or lying on branches.

IN BRIEF **Class:** *Reptiles* **Order:** *Scaled reptiles*
Suborder: *Lizards* **Family:** *Skinks* **Range:** *Solomon Islands (archipelago)*

Pueblan Milk Snake

Lampropeltis triangulum campbelli

Terrarium type: 🏔️🌲
Level of difficulty: 1
Activity: ☀️ 🌙
Habit: 🌿🌿

Characteristics: TL about 36 inches (90 cm). To ascertain sex, see page 15.
Terrarium: Woodland terrarium with branches to climb on and places to hide. Substrate: mixture of sandy soil with peat and leaves. Sufficiently large bathing pan. Recommended terrarium size for housing an adult pair: 36 × 17 × 17 inches (90 × 45 × 45 cm). To keep a third specimen, increase area by 20%. Air temperature 70–81°F (21–27°C), at night 61–71.5°F (16–22°C), water temperature 64.5–68°F (18–20°C), basking islands 86°F (30°C). Atmospheric humidity 50–70%. Lighting: 12 hours.
Keeping/Care: Because of cannibalism, it is advisable to keep a pair or a group only if the animals are the same size. They should be fed separately. In winter, lower temperature by 7°F (4°C) day and night; lighting: 6 hours.
Diet: Mice or rats of the appropriate size.
Behavior: Peaceful animals where terrarium keeper is concerned. They hide in crevices or under rocks and pieces of wood in the daytime.

IN BRIEF **Class:** *Reptiles* **Order:** *Scaled reptiles* **Suborder:** *Snakes* **Family:** *Colubrids* **Range:** *Mexican states of Puebla, Morelos, and Oaxaca. Many milk snakes are uneasy when handled.*

Razorback Musk Turtle

Sternotherus carinatus

Also: *Kinosternum carinatum*

Characteristics: CL up to 7¼ inches (18 cm). Males larger, with more massive head and thicker tail.

Terrarium type: ⌒

Level of difficulty: 1

Activity: ☼

Habit: ◐

Terrarium: Aquatic terrarium with ¾ water portion and water level of about 6 inches (15 cm). Maintain good water quality. Provide hiding places and visual barriers in the form of cork or clay tubes, stones, or roots above and below the water. Recommended minimum size of a terrarium (length × width) for housing an adult pair: 32 × 16 inches (80 × 40 cm). Air temperature 81–84.5°F (27–29°C), at night 64.5–71.5°F (18–22°C), water temperature 77–79°F (25–26°C), basking islands 95–104°F (35–40°C). Lighting: up to 12 hours. UV radiation required.

Keeping/Care: Keep as a group with one male and several females. In the summer months, can be kept outdoors in a pond. Hibernation: 8–10 weeks at 50°F (10°C).

Diet: Earthworms, insects, snails, and pieces of fish. Gelatin-based foods and dry foods for aquatic turtles, mineral supplementation.

Behavior: These turtles prefer to stay in the water, but also enjoy basking.

IN BRIEF **Class:** *Reptiles* **Order:** *Tortoises and turtles* **Suborder:** *Common-necked or straight-necked turtles* **Family:** *Mud and musk turtles* **Range:** *Southeastern United States*

Red-banded Rubber Frog

Phrynomerus bifasciatus

Also: Red-banded frog, banded rubber frog

Characteristics: SVL up to 1⅝ inches (4 cm). Males smaller, with black throats.

Terrarium type: 🌱

Level of difficulty: 1 !

Activity: ☽

Habit: 〰

Terrarium: Rainforest terrarium with dense plantings and hiding places under cork bark, flat stones, and roots. Supply water dish. Recommended terrarium size for housing an adult pair: 24 × 16 × 16 inches (60 × 40 × 40 cm). Air temperature 71.5–79°F (22–26°C), at night 64.5–68°F (18–20°C). Atmospheric humidity in the daytime 60–80%, at night over 90%. Lighting: 10–12 hours.

Keeping/Care: Colors fade if lighting is too bright. Breeding most successful in small groups. Caution: Because of toxins in their skin you may experience skin irritations after touching these animals.

Diet: Flies, small house crickets, field crickets or grasshoppers, wax moths, and small earthworms.

Behavior: Mainly nocturnal. Terrestrial, but also found on banana plants and in hollow trees. The species runs on all fours and can easily turn its neck and head to the side.

IN BRIEF **Class:** *Amphibians* **Order:** *Frogs and toads*
Suborder: *Modern or advanced frogs* **Family:** *Narrowmouth or microhylid frogs* **Range:** *South of the Congo to Namibia*

Red-eared Slider

Trachemys scripta elegans

Also: *Pseudemys scripta elegans*
Characteristics: CL up to 12 inches (30 cm). Males smaller, with bigger tails, and larger claws on front legs.

Terrarium type: 〰
Level of difficulty: 1
Activity: ☼
Habit: ◌ ⟱

Terrarium: Aquatic terrarium with ⅔ water portion. Water level deep enough for swimming. Clean water regularly. Can be kept in garden pond, but the pond must be surrounded with a good fence because of the danger of escape. Recommended minimum size of a terrarium (length × width) for housing an adult pair: 64 × 32 inches (160 × 80 cm). Air temperature 77–86°F (25–30°C), at night 71.6°F (22°C), water temperature 77°F (25°C), basking islands up to 104°F (40°C). Lighting: up to 12 hours. UV radiation required.
Keeping/Care: Sensitive to drafts. Can be kept as a pair and, after testing compatibility, as a group with several females. Hibernation: 8–12 weeks at 50–59°F (8–15°C).
Diet: Omnivorous. Gelatin-based foods and dry foods for aquatic turtles are readily accepted. Also worms, fish, romaine lettuce, and water plants. Less carnivorous with age.
Behavior: Usually stay in and near bodies of water. Rapid growth.
Similar needs: Cumberland slider, *Chrysemys scripta troosti*

IN BRIEF **Class:** *Reptiles* **Order:** *Tortoises and turtles*
Suborder: *Common-necked or straight-necked turtles* **Family:**
Pond and box turtles **Range:** *For this species, southeastern quarter of United States, south to Brazil; for this subspecies, Mississippi valley of United States south to Gulf of Mexico* 199

Red-eyed Tree Frog

Agalychnis callidryas

Also: Red-eyed leaf frog, gaudy leaf frog

Characteristics: SVL up to 2⅞ inches (7 cm). Males are about ⅛ smaller.

Terrarium type: ◠

Level of difficulty: 2

Activity: ☽

Habit: ↟↟

Terrarium: Rainforest terrarium with water container about 4 inches (10 cm) deep. Use humus or peat as substrate. Decorate with large-leaved, stable plants and climbing branches. Recommended terrarium size for housing an adult pair: (24 × 16 × 28 inches (60 × 40 × 70 cm). Temperature 71.5–82.5°F (22–28°C), at night 64.5–68°F (18–20°C), water temperature 77°F (25°C). Atmospheric humidity 50–70%, at night up to 95%. Lighting: 10–12 hours.

Keeping/Care: These frogs get along well together. For breeding, keep one male with one or more females and simulate rainy season in winter. Eggs are laid on leaves hanging over water. They die quickly if living conditions are not sufficiently hygienic.

Diet: Field crickets, flies, and wax moths.

Behavior: During the day, these frogs sleep hunched up, attached to the undersides of leaves. They are good climbers, as their opposable thumbs and suction cups at tips of toes help them hold on to branches.

IN BRIEF **Class:** *Amphibians* **Order:** *Frogs and toads* **Suborder:** *Modern or advanced frogs* **Family:** *New World tree frogs* **Range:** *Rainforests from Mexico to Panama*

Redfoot Tortoise

Chelonoidis carbonaria

Also: *Geochelone carbonaria, Testudo carbonaria*

Characteristics: CL up to 20 inches (50 cm). Males have concave plastron (see page 26), longer and thicker tail.

Terrarium type: [icon]
Level of difficulty: 2
Activity: [icon]
Habit: [icon]

Terrarium: Rainforest terrarium. Provide leaf-mold substrate, basking place, and water dish for drinking and bathing. Recommended minimum size (length × width) for a terrarium housing an adult pair: 160 × 80 inches (400 × 200 cm). Increase by 10% each for third and fourth specimens, then by 20% for each additional specimen. Temperature 75–90°F (24–32°C), at night 68–71.5°F (20–22°C), basking islands 104–113°F (40–45°C). Atmospheric humidity 80–90%. Lighting: 12–14 hours. UV radiation required.

Keeping/Care: After testing compatibility, can be kept as a group. Keep outdoors in summer if air is warm and humid enough. Places in sun and shade, as well as a rainproof shelter, are needed.

Diet: Dandelions, clover, romaine lettuce, and vegetables, as well as fish, meat, and small dead rodents. Offer fruit once a week at most. Calcium-containing food supplements on a regular basis.

Behavior: Becomes ill if atmospheric humidity is too low.

IN BRIEF **Class:** *Reptiles* **Order:** *Scaled reptiles*
Suborder: *Common-necked or straight-necked turtles*
Family: *Tortoises* **Range:** *Venezuela to Argentina*

Red-headed Rock Agama

Agama agama

Also: Common agama, rainbow agama

Characteristics: Depending on sub-species, TL 14–16 inches (35–40 cm), SVL 4–5¼ inches (10–13 cm). Males bigger, more brightly colored, with larger preanal pores (see page 27).

Terrarium type:

Level of difficulty: 2

Activity:

Habit:

Terrarium: Roomy dry terrarium with sandy substrate. Provide climbing and hiding places. Heat with cable heating or heat mats. May be planted with robust species in unheated portion of substrate. Recommended terrarium size for housing an adult pair: 72 × 40 × 32 inches (180 × 100 × 80 cm). Mist terrarium 2–3 times per week. Temperature 86–95°F (30–35°C), at night 64.5–68°F (18–20°C), basking islands 104–113°F (40–45°C). Atmospheric humidity 50–70%. Ranges may differ, depending on subspecies. Lighting: up to 14 hours. UV radiation required.

Keeping/Care: Keep as a pair or as a group with one male. Lots of warmth, very bright light, and reduced temperature at night very important.

Diet: House crickets, cockroaches, worms, pinkie mice. Provide mineral supplementation.

Behavior: Ground dweller, but enjoys climbing. Lives in groups.

IN BRIEF **Class:** *Reptiles* **Order:** *Scaled reptiles* **Suborder:** *Lizards* **Family:** *Agamas* **Range:** *Central to southern Africa*

Red-legged Pan Frog

Kassina maculata

Also: Brown-spotted tree frog, spotted running frog, *Hylambates maculates*

Terrarium type: 〰 🌿
Level of difficulty: 1
Activity: ☽
Habit: 🔀

Characteristics: SVL up to 3¼ inches (8 cm). Males stay slightly smaller, with yellowish throat.

Terrarium: Rainforest terrarium with large water dish; water level 2–4 inches (5–10 cm). Create gentle slope to access land area or provide landing place. Substrate should hold moisture well: peat/sphagnum mixture, for example. Branches for climbing and plants as hiding places, as well as retreats under roots and in cork tubes. Recommended terrarium size for housing an adult pair: 24 × 24 × 24 inches (60 × 60 × 60 cm). Air temperature 71.5–81°F (22–27°C), at night 64.5–68°F (18–20°C), water temperature 77°F (25°C). Atmospheric humidity 60–70%. Lighting: 12–14 hours.

Keeping/Care: Males compete for places to call from. Keep only specimens of the same size together.

Diet: Flies, wax moth larvae, house crickets, field crickets, grasshoppers, and cockroaches.

Behavior: Once used to the terrarium, the frogs sometimes will hunt for food even in the daytime.

IN BRIEF **Class:** *Amphibians* **Order:** *Frogs and toads* **Suborder:** *Modern or advanced frogs* **Family:** *African tree frogs* **Range:** *Western Africa, central to southern Africa*

Red-sided Garter Snake

Thamnophis sirtalis parietalis

Characteristics: TL up to 48 inches (120 cm). To ascertain sex, see page 15.

Terrarium: Dry woodland terrarium with large bathing pan. Provide places to bask, places to hide and climb. Recommended terrarium size for housing an adult pair: 60 × 36 × 30 inches (150 × 90 × 75 cm). For each additional specimen, add 20% to area. Air temperature 77–82.5°F (25–28°C), at night 61–68°F (16–20°C), water temperature 77°F (25°C), basking islands 86°F (30°C). Values can be less or more, depending on origin. Atmospheric humidity 50–60%. Lighting: 12 hours, partly UV.

Keeping/Care: Can be kept as a group, as these snakes get along well together. Make sure terrarium is escape-proof. Hibernation: 2–3 months at 50–59°F (10–15°C), specimens of northern origin at 46.5–50°F (8–10°C).

Diet: Earthworms, fish, or pinkie mice. Best to feed at midday, the time the species looks for food in the wild as well.

Behavior: These snakes like to bask and soak. They need peace and quiet and are quite shy. Newly captured specimens may bite and excrete a foul-smelling musk.

Terrarium type: 〰️ 🌿
Level of difficulty: 1
Activity: ☀️
Habit: 🔽

IN BRIEF **Class:** *Reptiles* **Order:** *Scaled reptiles* **Suborder:** *Snakes* **Family:** *Colubrids* **Range:** *South central Canada to northern Texas*

Red-spotted Newt

Notophthalmus viridescens

Terrarium type: ⬜⬜ ⬜
Level of difficulty: 1
Activity: ⬜ ⬜
Habit: ⬜ ⬜

Characteristics: TL, 2⅞–5½ inches (7–14 cm), SVL 1½–2⅞ inches (3.5–7 cm). Males display nuptial pads (see page 26) in breeding condition, a higher crest, and a swollen, rounded cloaca (conical in females).

Terrarium: Moist woodland terrarium with hiding places for the land form (eft), aquarium for the larval form and adult form (see Behavior). Recommended terrarium size for housing an adult pair: 20 × 12 × 12 inches (50 × 30 × 30 cm); 25% more for each additional specimen. Temperature for northern subspecies to 68°F (20°C), for southern subspecies to 75°F (24°C). Atmospheric humidity by day to 80%, at night over 90%. Low lighting: 10 hours.

Keeping/Care: Keep animals of the same size as a pair or as a group. Hibernation: northern species, 8–10 weeks at 43°F (6°C), southern species at 50°F (10°C).

Diet: Land form: slugs, worms, insects. Aquatic form: small crustaceans and larvae of aquatic insects, small worms, frozen bloodworms.

Behavior: Aquatic in larval stage. As red-colored efts, crepuscular and terrestrial for up to 3 years. In adult stage, diurnal and aquatic, with green coloring.

IN BRIEF **Class:** *Amphibians* **Order:** *Salamanders*
Suborder: *Salamanders and their allies* **Family:** *Salamanders and newts* **Range:** *Canada to Mexico*

Reeves' Turtle

Chinemys reevesii

Characteristics: CL up to 6¾ inches (17 cm). Males ⅓ smaller and darker. Plastron slightly concave (see page 26).

Terrarium type: ⌇
Level of difficulty: 1
Activity: ☼
Habit: ◌ ⩳

Terrarium: Aquatic terrarium with ⅔ water portion and water level that is twice the CL. Recommended minimum area of a terrarium (length × width) housing an adult pair: 32 × 16 inches (80 × 40 cm). Air and water temperature 77°F (25°C), at night 68°F (20°C), basking islands about 86°F (30°C). Lighting: up to 12 hours. UV radiation required.

Keeping/Care: Keep as a pair or, after testing compatibility, as a group with several females. Maintain good water quality. Can be kept outdoors in summer months. When housed outdoors, this species buries itself in the land portion at times. Hibernation: 7–10 weeks at 59°F (15°C).

Diet: Small fish, pieces of fish, crustaceans, plain gelatin-based mixtures, dry food for aquatic turtles, and mineral supplements.

Behavior: Aquatic species that regularly visits the land portion to dry off or to bask. These animals are peaceful and quickly become friendly.

IN BRIEF **Class:** *Reptiles* **Order:** *Tortoises and turtles* **Suborder:** *Common-necked or straight-necked turtles* **Family:** *Old World freshwater turtles* **Range:** *China, Japan, and the Philippines*

Reticulated Python

Python reticulatus

Terrarium type: 🗠
Level of difficulty: 3
Activity: 🌑 🌙
Habit: 🌱

Characteristics: TL 240 inches (600 cm), rarely over 320 inches (800 cm), up to maximum of about 400 inches (1,000 cm). To ascertain sex, see page 15.

Terrarium: Woodland terrarium with strong branches for climbing, large water pan, and hiding places on the ground. Recommended terrarium size for housing an adult pair up to 100 inches (250 cm): 100 × 48 × 72 inches (250 × 120 × 180 cm); larger specimens need proportionately larger quarters. Air temperature 77–90°F (25–32°C), at night 71.5–75°F (22–24°C), water temperature 75–79°F (24–26°C), basking islands 95–104°F (35–40°C). Atmospheric humidity 60–70%, at night 80–90%. Lighting: 12–14 hours.

Keeping/Care: The species is known to go long periods without eating. Most specimens have irascible dispositions. They grow rapidly. Do not get a small specimen unless you will have room to house it as an adult!

Diet: Depending on size, rats, guinea pigs, rabbits, doves, chickens, and ducks.

Behavior: Primarily crepuscular and nocturnal. Predominantly ground dwellers, but fond of climbing and soaking. Lively, but also more aggressive than many other pythons.

IN BRIEF **Class:** *Reptiles* **Order:** *Scaled reptiles*
Suborder: *Snakes* **Family:** *Boas and pythons* **Range:** *Burma, Thailand, Laos, Cambodia, Vietnam, Malaysia, Indonesia, and the Philippines*

Rough Green Snake

Opheodrys aestivus

Characteristics: TL 32 inches (80 cm), rarely 46 inches (115 cm). Females generally longer. Males have longer tail and larger number of subcaudal scales (larger scales on the underside of the tail).

Terrarium type: 🌲🌲
Level of difficulty: 2
Activity: ☀️
Habit: 🌿 🌳

Terrarium: Woodland terrarium with climbing branches and places to hide and retreat in dense plantings. Small water dish is adequate. Cover substrate with moss and leaves. Recommended terrarium size for housing an adult pair up to 32 inches (80 cm) long: 32 × 16 × 32 inches (80 × 40 × 80 cm). Air temperature 77–86°F (25–30°C), at night 59–68°F (15–20°C), water temperature same as air, basking islands 95°F (35°C). Atmospheric humidity 60–70%. Lighting: 12–14 hours, partly UV.

Keeping/Care: Can be kept as a group, but the snakes easily become stressed if population is too large. Ventilate well. Sensitive to stale air and drafts. Hibernation: 3 months at 46.5–59°F (8–15°C).

Diet: Grasshoppers, field crickets, caterpillars, and spiders.

Behavior: Moves very quickly. Remains still when approached. Virtually invisible when resting on vines. Bites only rarely.

IN BRIEF **Class:** *Reptiles* **Order:** *Scaled reptiles* **Suborder:** *Snakes* **Family:** *Colubrids* **Range:** *Southeastern United States to northeastern Mexico*

Round-tailed Horned Lizard

Phrynosoma modestum

Terrarium type: 🌵
Level of difficulty: 3
Activity: ☀
Habit: ☷

Characteristics: TL 3¼–4 inches (8–10 cm), SVL 1⅝–2½ inches (4–6 cm). Females slightly smaller, with shorter tail.

Terrarium: Dry terrarium with sand and gravel substrate, about 4–6 inches (10–15 cm) deep, kept slightly damp in one corner. Mist lightly 2–3 times weekly. Provide hiding places under stones and pieces of roots. Plant with succulents. Recommended terrarium size for housing an adult pair: 24 × 16 × 16 inches (60 × 40 × 40 cm). Temperature 86–104°F (30–40°C), at night 64.5–68°F (18–20°C), basking islands 113°F (45°C). Atmospheric humidity less than 50%. Bright lighting: 14 hours. UV radiation required.

Keeping/Care: Keep as a pair or as a group with only one male. Because of their specialized dietary and environmental requirements horned lizards are not recommended as pets.

Diet: Large ants are its main diet. Some will accept mealworms, flies, crickets, wax moths and their larvae.

Behavior: Obtains most of its water through the food it eats, but laps dew.

IN BRIEF **Class:** *Reptiles* **Order:** *Scaled reptiles* **Suborder:** *Lizards* **Family:** *Iguanas* **Range:** *Southeastern Arizona, New Mexico, western Texas to Mexico*

Russian Tortoise

Agrionemys horsfieldii

Also: Fourtoe tortoise

Characteristics: CL up to 11¼ inches (28 cm). Males smaller, with bigger tails.

Terrarium type: 🌵 🏔️
Level of difficulty: 2
Activity: ☀️
Habit: ⬇️

Terrarium: Dry terrarium. Recommended minimum area of terrarium or outdoor pen (length × width) for housing an adult pair: 96 × 48 inches (240 × 120 cm). Add 10% each for third and fourth specimens, then 20% for each additional tortoise. Temperature 77–95°F (25–35°C), at night 50–59°F (10–15°C), basking islands about 113°F (45°C). Atmospheric humidity 40–75%. Lighting: up to 12 hours. UV radiation and spotlight for dreary days required.

Keeping/Care: After compatibility test, may be kept as a group. Can be kept outdoors in summer. Shade-giving plants, sunny places, and waterproof shelter required. Replace water in drinking and bathing dish daily. After slow lowering of temperature, 2–3 months of hibernation at 41–50°F (5–10°C).

Diet: Dandelions, clover, romaine lettuce, and chopped vegetables. Calcium-containing supplement on a regular basis.

Behavior: Likes to bury itself in the ground for several weeks. Sensitive to damp, cool weather.

IN BRIEF **Class:** *Reptiles* **Order:** *Tortoises and turtles*
Suborder: *Common-necked or straight-necked turtles*
Family: *Tortoises* **Range:** *Steppes of Central Asia*

Sand Monitor

Varanus flavirufus

Also: *Varanus gouldii,* **Gould's monitor**

Characteristics: TL 64 inches (160 cm), SVL up to 26 inches (65 cm). Males have longer heads; females stay 20% smaller.

Terrarium type: 🌵
Level of difficulty: 2
Activity: ☀
Habit: ⬇⬇

Terrarium: Dry terrarium with firm layer of loam and sand substrate 8–12 inches (20–30 cm) deep and with well-anchored decorations that can't be toppled by digging activity. Provide basking places, cooler retreats, and climbing areas. Water portion deep enough for submersion. Recommended terrarium size for housing an adult pair: 160 × 80 × 80 inches (400 × 200 × 200 cm). Add 15% to area for each additional female. Temperature 81–91.5°F (27–33°C), at night 64.5–71.5°F (18–22°C), basking islands 104°F (40°C). Atmospheric humidity 50–70%. Lighting: 14 hours. UV radiation required.

Keeping/Care: Keep as single animal, a pair, or a group with one male. Hibernation not necessary, but stimulates reproduction.

Diet: Large insects, chicks, mice, small rats, and mineral supplements. Because of tendency to obesity, do not overfeed

Behavior: Lively ground dweller that likes to dig. Defends itself by biting and lashing out with its tail.

IN BRIEF **Class:** *Reptiles* **Order:** *Scaled reptiles* **Suborder:** *Lizards* **Family:** *Monitor lizards* **Range:** *Australia and southern New Guinea*

Savannah Monitor Lizard

Varanus exanthematicus

Characteristics: TL 51 inches (130 cm), rarely 60 inches (150 cm), SVL up to 28 inches (70 cm). Sex can be ascertained only by endoscopy, performed by veterinarian.

Terrarium type: 🌵
Level of difficulty: 2
Activity: ☀️
Habit: 〰️

Terrarium: Dry terrarium. Substrate: loam and sand, suitable for digging. Drinking bowl must be supplied. Provide basking places, as well as retreats under piles of stones, roots, and in cork tubes. Recommended terrarium size for housing an adult pair: 168 × 80 × 80 inches (420 × 200 × 200 cm). Temperature 82.5–95°F (28–35°C), at night 68°F (20°C), basking islands 104–113°F (40–45°C). Atmospheric humidity 60–70%. Lighting: 14 hours. UV radiation required.

Keeping/Care: Keep singly or as a pair. Hibernation: 8–12 weeks at 59°F (15°C).

Diet: Large insects, beetles, snails, earthworms, *Zophobas* larvae, wax moth larvae, pinkie mice and rats, and eggs. Occasionally fast for several days.

Behavior: Captive-bred animals can be quite tame. Always be cautious around monitor lizards; they can bite hard and lash out with their tails.

IN BRIEF **Class:** *Reptiles* **Order:** *Scaled reptiles* **Suborder:** *Lizards* **Family:** *Monitor lizards* **Range:** *Central Africa, from Senegal to Ethiopia*

Schneider's Skink

Novoeumeces schneideri

Also: *Eumeces schneideri*
Characteristics: TL 14½ inches (36 cm), SVL up to 9½ inches (24 cm). Males are bigger and more brightly colored. The females sometimes lack the orange marking.

Terrarium type: 🌵
Level of difficulty: 1
Activity: ☀
Habit: 〰

Terrarium: Desert terrarium with substrate suitable for digging, 3¼–4 inches (8–10 cm) deep. Use flat stone slabs to create hiding places. Plants in pots are best. Recommended terrarium size for housing an adult pair: 60 × 40 × 24 inches (150 × 100 × 60 cm). Temperature 82.5–90°F (28–32°C), at night 68°F (20°C), basking islands 95–104°F (35–40°C). Lighting: 12–14 hours. UV radiation required.

Keeping/Care: Keep as a pair. In winter, reduce temperature by 50°F (10°C) for 6–8 weeks and lighting to 6–8 hours.

Diet: Grasshoppers, field crickets, house crickets, snails, pinkie mice, rats; soft fruit and vegetables.

Behavior: These skinks live in seclusion and like to bury themselves in sand. The females practice brood care; they guard the clutch and keep the eggs damp with their urine.

Similar needs: Berber skink (*Novoeumeces algeriensis*).

IN BRIEF **Class:** *Reptiles* **Order:** *Scaled reptiles* **Suborder:** *Lizards* **Family:** *Skinks* **Range:** *Northeastern Africa to northwestern India*

Senegal Running Frog

Kassina senegalensis

Also: Bubbling kassina

Characteristics: SVL up to 1¾ inches (4.5 cm). Males stay slightly smaller and have dark throats.

Terrarium type:
Level of difficulty: 1
Activity:
Habit:

Terrarium: Semidry terrarium with 1¼–1⅝ inches (3–4 cm) of moisture-retaining substrate, kept slightly moist by daily misting. Provide hiding places under cork bark, flat stones, and roots. Supply water dish for bathing and drinking. Recommended terrarium size for housing an adult pair: 24 × 16 × 16 inches (60 × 40 × 40 cm). Air temperature 71.5–82.5°F (22–28°C), at night 64.5–68°F (18–20°C). Atmospheric humidity 40–70%. Lighting: 10–12 hours.

Keeping/Care: Because of potential cannibalism, keep only animals of the same size. If intimidated by more dominant specimens, they often starve.

Diet: Flies, wax moths, mealworms, earthworms, small house crickets, field crickets, and grasshoppers. Vitamin/mineral supplements or gut-load insects prior to feeding.

Behavior: Instead of hopping, these frogs more or less walk or run.

Similar needs: *Kassina wealii*

IN BRIEF **Class:** *Amphibians* **Order:** *Frogs and toads* **Suborder:** *Modern or advanced frogs* **Family:** *African tree frogs* **Range:** *Central Africa*

Shingleback Skink

Also: Pinecone lizard, stumpy-tailed lizard, *Trachysaurus rugosus*
Characteristics: TL 14.5 inches (37 cm), SVL 11 inches (28 cm). Males have bigger, wider heads and longer, more pointed tails.

Terrarium type: 🌵
Level of difficulty: 1
Activity: ☀
Habit: 〰

Terrarium: Savannah terrarium with substrate 3¼–4 inches (8–10 cm) deep, suitable for digging. Create hiding places under flat stone slabs or piles of stones. Provide roots and climbing branches. Plants in pots are best. Recommended terrarium size for housing an adult pair: 68 × 44 × 36 inches (170 × 110 × 90 cm). Temperature 71.5–86°F (22–30°C), at night 64.5–68°F (18–20°C), basking islands 95–104°F (35–40°C). Atmospheric humidity 60%. Lighting: 12–14 hours. UV radiation required.

Keeping/Care: Can also be kept as a group with different sexes. In winter, lower temperature to 50–59°F (10–15°C) for 8–12 weeks.

Diet: Omnivorous; chopped greens and vegetables, soft fruit, and animal foods such as field crickets and baby rodents. Mineral supplements recommended.

Behavior: These skinks defend themselves by opening their mouths, hissing, and displaying their blue tongues; they can bite hard. Predators are possibly confused by the tail resembling the head.

IN BRIEF **Class:** *Reptiles* **Order:** *Scaled reptiles*
Suborder: *Lizards* **Family:** *Skinks* **Range:** *Australia, Tasmania, New Guinea, Indonesia*

Sinaloan Milk Snake

Lampropeltis triangulum sinaloae

Characteristics: TL about 50 inches (125 cm). To ascertain sex, see page 15.

Terrarium: Woodland terrarium with hiding places such as pieces of bark and rocks. Equipping the terrarium with a container of drinking water is essential. Recommended terrarium size for housing an adult pair: 48 × 24 × 24 inches (120 × 60 × 60 cm). To keep a third specimen, increase area by 20%. Air temperature 79–91.5°F (26–33°C), at night 64.5–77°F (18–25°C), water temperature same as air. Basking islands up to 95°F (35°C). Atmospheric humidity 50–60%. Lighting: 12 hours.

Keeping/Care: Because of cannibalism, keeping a pair or a group is recommended only if the animals are the same size and are fed individually. In winter, lower temperature by 11°F (6°C) both day and night; reduce lighting period to 6 hours.

Diet: Mice or rats of the appropriate size.

Behavior: Very peaceful animals, predominantly crepuscular and nocturnal. In the daytime, the species hides in crevices or under rocks and wood.

Terrarium type:
Level of difficulty: 1
Activity:
Habit:

IN BRIEF **Class:** *Reptiles* **Order:** *Scaled reptiles* **Suborder:** *Snakes* **Family:** *Colubrids* **Range:** *Mexican states of Sonora, Chihuahua, and Sinaloa. Captive-raised specimens are generally sold.*

Six-lined Grass Lizard

Takydromus sexlineatus

Terrarium type:	🌿🌿
Level of difficulty:	1
Activity:	☀️
Habit:	🌱

Characteristics: TL 14½ inches (36 cm), SVL up to 2½ inches (6 cm). Males have thickened tail base, larger femoral pores (see page 26), and a row of black-edged, yellowish spots from the snout tip to the tail base.

Terrarium: Woodland terrarium. Decorate with plants as long-stemmed as possible, dry, not overly thick twigs, vines, and roots. Recommended terrarium size for housing an adult pair: 32 × 16 × 24 inches (80 × 40 × 60 cm). Temperature 79–82.5°F (26–28°C), at night 68–71.5°F (20–22°C), basking islands 86–95°F (30–35°C). Atmospheric humidity 60–80%. Lighting: 10–12 hours. UV radiation required.

Keeping/Care: Keep as a pair or as a group with only one male. Hibernation: 8 weeks at 71.5–75°F (22–24°C).

Diet: Flies such as *Drosophila* and blowflies, mealworm larvae and adults, small grasshoppers, house crickets, field crickets, and spiders.

Behavior: Very active. The long tail helps the lizard keep its balance. If tail is grabbed, it will break off.

IN BRIEF **Class:** *Reptiles:* **Order:** *Scaled reptiles* **Suborder:** *Lizards* **Family:** *Wall lizards* **Range:** *Southern China, Vietnam, Indochina, Malaysia, and Indonesia*

South African Rock Scorpion

Hadogenes bicolor

Also: Flat rock scorpion

Characteristics: TL up to 6¾ inches (17 cm). Males are darker in color and have, in comparison with females, unusually long metasomal segments (see page 27).

Terrarium type: 🌵
Level of difficulty: 1 !
Activity: ☽
Habit:

Terrarium: Dry terrarium, with substrate 2–4 inches (5–10 cm) deep: mixture of sand, soil, and leaves. Carefully arranged and stable stacks of flat rocks or slate as hiding places. A shallow drinking bowl is essential. Recommended terrarium size for one adult: 16 × 12 × 12 inches (40 × 30 × 30 cm). Temperature 82.5–86°F (28–30°C), at night 71.5°F (22°C). Atmospheric humidity 60–80%. Lighting: 8–10 hours.

Keeping/Care: Keep the sexes singly. Mist lightly every couple of weeks or less. This is among the least poisonous of scorpion species; the sting is only briefly painful and is no more dangerous than a mild wasp sting.

Diet: House crickets, field crickets, grasshoppers, cockroaches, mealworms, beetles, and *Zophobas* larvae.

Behavior: Its docile nature and nondangerous sting makes it a good beginner's scorpion.

IN BRIEF **Class:** *Arachnids* **Order:** *Scorpions*
Suborder: *Neoscorpionina* **Family:** *Ischnuridae*
Range: *South Africa*

Southern Long-tailed Lizard

Latastia longicaudata

Also: Red sand ameiva, African long-tailed lizard

Characteristics: TL up to 16 inches (40 cm), SVL 4⅜ inches (11 cm). Hard to sex. Males usually larger.

Terrarium type: 〰
Level of difficulty: 2
Activity: ☼
Habit: ⬇⬇ ◇

Terrarium: Dry terrarium with sand-and-loam substrate suitable for digging. Keep bottom layer slightly moist. Provide hiding places under flat stones, roots, and pieces of cork, as well as climbing areas. Recommended terrarium size for housing an adult pair: 32 × 16 × 16 inches (80 × 40 × 40 cm). Temperature 82.5–95°F (28–34°C), at night 64.5–71.5°F (18–22°C), basking islands up to 104°F (40°C). Atmospheric humidity 50–60%. Lighting: 12–14 hours. UV radiation required.

Keeping/Care: Keep as a pair or as a group with one male. Hibernation: 4–6 weeks at 53.5–61°F (12–16°C).

Diet: Grasshoppers, field crickets, house crickets, cockroaches, mealworms, and wax moths and their larvae. Mineral supplementation or gut-load insects.

Behavior: These lizards are fond of digging, but hide before midday heat or during the night, also in hollow trees.

IN BRIEF **Class:** *Reptiles* **Order:** *Scaled reptiles* **Suborder:** *Lizards* **Family:** *Wall lizards* **Range:** *North to East Africa from Egypt to Tanzania, and Arabian peninsula to Yemen*

Southern Painted Turtle

Chrysemys picta dorsalis

Characteristics: CL up to 6 inches (15 cm). Males ⅓ smaller, with longer tails and longer claws on forelimbs. Plastrons slightly concave.

Terrarium type: 〰
Level of difficulty: 1
Activity: ☼
Habit: ⬇ ◌

Terrarium: Aquatic terrarium with ⅔ water portion, water level twice the CL. Recommended minimum size of a terrarium (length × width) for housing an adult pair: 32 × 16 inches (80 × 40 cm). Air temperature 77–86°F (25–30°C), at night 59–68°F (15–20°C), water temperature 77°F (25°C), basking islands about 104°F (40°C). Lighting: 12–14 hours, UV radiation required.

Keeping/Care: Keep as a pair or, after compatibility test, as a group with several females. Can be kept outdoors in summer. Hibernation for northern species, 6–8 weeks at 50–59°F (10–15°C); for southern species, none is required.

Diet: Ominivore. Aquatic and marsh plants, small fish, pieces of fish, crustaceans, earthworms, insects, gelatin-based foods, dry foods for aquatic turtles, and mineral supplements.

Behavior: These turtles like to bask on branches or stones jutting out of the water.

IN BRIEF **Class:** *Reptiles* **Order:** *Tortoises and turtles* **Suborder:** *Common-necked or straight-necked turtles* **Family:** *Pond and box turtles* **Range:** *Southern Mississippi valley to Gulf of Mexico*

Spanish Ribbed Newt

Pleurodeles waltl

Characteristics: TL up to 12 inches (30 cm), SVL 4–6 inches (10–15 cm). Males smaller, slimmer, with longer tails. During mating season they display swollen cloacas and nuptial pads (see page 26).

Terrarium type: ⌒
Level of difficulty: 1
Activity: ☀ ☾
Habit: ⌄⌄ ◯

Terrarium: Aquatic terrarium with 50% land portion and water level of 4–6 inches (10–15 cm). Substrate of water portion: gravel; for land portion, use soil covered with moss. Provide hiding places under roots and cork. Adequate terrarium size for an adult pair: 32 × 14 × 16 inches (80 × 35 × 40 cm); for up to 6 specimens: 40 × 16 × 20 inches (100 × 40 × 50 cm). Air temperature 63–68°F (17–20°C), at night 59°F (15°C), water temperature 64.5–71.5°F (18–22°C). Lighting: 10–12 hours.

Keeping/Care: Specimens of roughly the same size can be kept as a group. Hibernation: 4–6 weeks at 43–50°F (7–10°C), with lighting reduced to 6 hours and water level raised to 10 inches (25 cm).

Diet: Slugs, earthworms, *Tubifex*, insects, small fish, pieces of fish and meat, and mineral supplements.

Behavior: Crepuscular and nocturnal; diurnal only during reproductive period.

IN BRIEF **Class:** *Amphibians* **Order:** *Salamanders* **Suborder:** *Salamanders and their allies* **Family:** *Salamanders and newts* **Range:** *Spain to Morocco*

Speckled Forest Skink

Mabuya macularia

Also: Bronze grass skink, spotted skink

Characteristics: TL 6¾ inches (17 cm), SVL up to 2¾ inches (7 cm). Males have pronounced hemipenal sacs and orange throat and chest.

Terrarium type: 🌵
Level of difficulty: 1
Activity: ☀
Habit:

Terrarium: Woodland terrarium with substrate 4–6 inches (10–15 cm) deep, suitable for digging. Plants in pots are best. Provide hiding places on the ground, in the form of flat stone slabs and cork tubes, and water bowl. Furnish with climbing branches and rear wall suitable for climbing. Recommended terrarium size for an adult pair: 32 × 16 × 20 inches (80 × 40 × 50 cm). Light one corner of terrarium brightly and keep it warmer. In the rest of the terrarium, temperature 75–79°F (24–26°C), at night 68°F (20°C), basking islands 86–90°F (30–32°C). Atmospheric humidity 50–70%. Lighting: 12–14 hours. UV radiation required.

Keeping/Care: Keep as a pair. Provide basking areas.

Diet: Grasshoppers, field crickets, house crickets, snails, and meadow plankton. Soft fruit.

Behavior: Quite aggressive species. Predominantly ground-dwelling, but also likes climbing.

Similar needs: *Mabuya multifasciata*

IN BRIEF **Class:** *Reptiles* **Order:** *Scaled reptiles* **Suborder:** *Lizards* **Family:** *Skinks* **Range:** *Pakistan to Indochina, northern Malaysia*

Spiny-tailed Monitor Lizard

Varanus acanthurus

Terrarium type: 🌵
Level of difficulty: 2
Activity: ☀
Habit: 🌙🔻 ⛰

Characteristics: TL 30 inches (75 cm), SVL up to 10 inches (25 cm). Hard to sex. Sex can be reliably ascertained only by endoscopy, performed by veterinarian.

Terrarium: Dry terrarium with stable piles of stones and hiding places. Substrate: deep, firm layer of loam and sand, 6–8 inches (15–20 cm) deep, as the species also digs. Basking places are important, as are cooler retreats. Recommended terrarium size for housing an adult pair: 60 × 24 × 40 inches (150 × 60 × 100 cm). Add 15% to area for each additional female. Temperature 77–86°F (25–30°C), at night 68°F (20°C), basking islands 104°F (40°C). Atmospheric humidity 50%. Lighting: 14 hours. UV radiation required.

Keeping/Care: Keep as a pair or in groups with one male. Hibernation not required, but it does stimulate breeding.

Diet: Large insects, mice, and small rats. Occasionally stop feeding for a few days, as the species tends to become overweight.

Behavior: Prefers to stay in rock crevices and under piles of stones.

IN BRIEF   **Class:** *Reptiles* **Order:** *Scaled reptiles*
Suborder: *Lizards* **Family:** *Monitor lizards* **Range:** *Northern, western, and central Australia*

Spotted Salamander

Ambystoma maculatum

Characteristics: TL 6–10 inches (15–25 cm). Males larger and slimmer. Identifiable by the slightly protruding cloacal opening during mating season.

Terrarium type: 〰
Level of difficulty: 1
Activity: ☼
Habit: ⬓

Terrarium: Aquatic terrarium with ⅕ water portion and water level of 4–6 inches (10–15 cm). Flat transition to land portion. Substrate: soil, humus, or peat covered with bark, rotten branches, leaves, and moss. Plant ivy and ferns. Recommended terrarium size for an adult pair: 32 × 14 × 16 inches (80 × 35 × 40 cm). Increase area by 25% for each additional specimen. Air and water temperature 63–70°F (17–21°C). Low lighting: 10 hours.

Keeping/Care: Keep a pair of animals of equal size or a group with one male and 3 females. Hibernation: 8–10 weeks at 41.5–46.5°F (5–8°C).

Diet: Earthworms, slugs, maggots, caterpillars, insects, spiders, and pillbugs.

Behavior: Makes burrows in the substrate and spends the day in these hiding places. Usually goes into the water only during reproductive period.

IN BRIEF **Class:** *Amphibians* **Order:** *Salamanders* **Suborder:** *Salamanders and their allies* **Family:** *Mole salamanders* **Range:** *Southeastern Canada through the central to eastern United States to northeastern Texas A very secretive species.*

Sudan Plated Lizard

Gerrhosaurus major

Also: tawny plated lizard, rough-scaled plated lizard

Characteristics: TL 22½ inches (56 cm), SVL 11¼ inches (28 cm). Males have larger femoral pores (see page 26).

Terrarium type: 🌵
Level of difficulty: 1
Activity: ☀
Habit: 🏜

Terrarium: Savannah terrarium with substrate 4–6 inches (10–15 cm) deep, suitable for digging; mixture of loam and sand. Furnish with stone slabs, roots, and branches that the lizards can use for climbing and as hiding places. Include robust plants in pots. Supply large bathing dish. Recommended terrarium size for housing an adult pair: 60 × 40 × 40 inches (150 × 100 × 100 cm). Temperature 82.5–95°F (28–35°C), at night 64.5–68°F (18–20°C), basking islands up to 113°F (45°C). Atmospheric humidity 50–60%. Lighting: up to 14 hours. UV radiation required.

Keeping/Care: Keep as a pair or as a group with one male. For breeding, 4–6 weeks of hibernation at 61–68°F (16–20°C).

Diet: Field crickets, house crickets, grasshoppers, cockroaches, snails, earthworms, small mammals, fruit, and vitamin/mineral supplements.

Behavior: Fond of digging, as well as basking. These lizards can become quite tame.

IN BRIEF **Class:** *Reptiles* **Order:** *Scaled reptiles*
Suborder: *Lizards* **Family:** *Spinytail or girdled lizards*
Range: *Eastern to southeastern Africa*

Surinam Toad

Pipa pipa

Characteristics: SVL 8 inches (20 cm). Males somewhat smaller, with vocal sacs and dark nuptial pads (see page 26) on their hind limbs.

Terrarium type: 〰️
Level of difficulty: 1
Activity: ☽
Habit: ⬦

Terrarium: Aquarium with low lighting. Provide roots or caves as hiding places. Substrate: fine gravel, 1¼ inches (3 cm) deep. Decorate tank with floating plants, as aquatic plants will be uprooted by the toads' swimming movements. Maintain good water quality. Recommended terrarium size for up to 3 adults: 40 × 16 × 20 inches (100 × 40 × 50 cm). Water temperature 77–86°F (25–30°C). Lighting: 10–12 hours.

Keeping/Care: These toads get along well together. If overfed, they become overweight quickly. The female incubates her eggs in pits or on her back. They hatch into miniature frogs.

Diet: Earthworms and small fish.

Behavior: These toads lie on the bottom waiting for prey, which they suck in like a vacuum cleaner. Found in slow-flowing to standing waters.

IN BRIEF **Class:** *Amphibians* **Order:** *Frogs and toads*
Suborder: *Ancient or primitive frogs* **Family:** *Tongueless frogs* **Range:** *Trinidad, Surinam to Peru*

Taiwan Beauty Snake

Orthriophis taeniurus frisei

Also: *Elaphe taeniura frisei*

Characteristics: TL 100 inches (250 cm), in rare cases even up to 120 inches (300 cm). Females usually somewhat longer. To ascertain sex, see page 15.

Terrarium type: 🗔
Level of difficulty: 1
Activity: ☼
Habit: ⤫⤫ 🌳

Terrarium: Slightly moist woodland terrarium with several hiding places on the ground, a large bathing pan, and branches for climbing. Recommended terrarium size for housing an adult pair: 100 × 50 × 88 inches (250 × 125 × 220 cm). To keep a third specimen, add 20% to the area. Air temperature 77–82.5°F (25–28°C), at night 71.5–75°F (22–24°C), water temperature 79°F (26°C), basking islands 86–90°F (30–32°C). Atmospheric humidity 60–80%. Lighting 10–12 hours, partly UV.

Keeping/Care: Several specimens can be housed together only if they are the same size, but they should be fed individually. Hibernation: December–February at 53.5–59°F (12–15°C).

Diet: Depending on size, mice or rats and chicks. Easily gets used to prekilled feeder animals.

Behavior: Good climber. Exhibits pronounced flight behavior.

IN BRIEF   **Class:** *Reptiles* **Order:** *Scaled reptiles*
Suborder: *Snakes* **Family:** *Colubrids* **Range:** *Taiwan*

Taveta Two-horned Chameleon

Bradypodion tavetanum

Also: Dwarf Fischer's chameleon

Characteristics: TL up to 8 inches (20 cm), SVL 3¼–3⅝ inches (8–9 cm). Females slightly smaller.

Terrarium type: 🔳
Level of difficulty: 3
Activity: ☀
Habit: 🌳

Terrarium: Woodland terrarium with lots of horizontal branches for climbing. Large ventilation areas are important for adequate supply of fresh air. Retreats and hiding places in dense plantings increase these animals' comfort level. Recommended terrarium size for housing an adult pair: 20 × 16 × 28 inches (50 × 40 × 70 cm). Temperature 71.5–79°F (22–26°C), at night 53.5–61°F (12–16°C). Atmospheric humidity 50%, at night 80%. Not overly bright lighting: 12 hours. UV radiation required.

Keeping/Care: Lowering temperature nightly very important. Territorial; keep singly except for mating attempts. To supply these lizards with water, mist daily or install a drip system.

Diet: Field crickets, house crickets, cockroaches, grasshoppers. Mineral supplements or gut-load feeder insects.

Behavior: Active, but shy and easily frightened. Dislikes bright lighting and warm temperatures.

IN BRIEF **Class:** *Reptiles* **Order:** *Scaled reptiles* **Suborder:** *Lizards* **Family:** *Chameleons* **Range:** *Kenya and Tanzania*

Thai Zebra Tarantula

Haplopelma albostriatum

Also: Thailand edible tarantula

Characteristics: Body up to 2½ inches (6 cm).

Terrarium type: 🔼🔼
Level of difficulty: 3 !
Activity: 🌅 🌙
Habit: 〰

Terrarium: Moist woodland terrarium with peat or humus substrate, 4 inches (10 cm) deep, kept slightly damp at all times. Provide pieces of bark as hiding places. Supply shallow water dish. Recommended terrarium size for one adult: 8 × 12 × 8 inches (20 × 30 × 20 cm). Temperature 71.5–77°F (22–25°C), at night 61–68°F (16–20°C). Atmospheric humidity 70–80%. Lighting: 8–10 hours.

Keeping/Care: Keep male or female singly. Perform work on the terrarium with care, as these tarantulas are easily irritated and will bite. Maintain good terrarium hygiene.

Diet: Depending on size, flies, wax moths, house crickets, grasshoppers, cockroaches, and baby mice.

Behavior: They live in burrows in the ground. When threatened, they raise their abdomens, display their chelicerae (see page 26), and drum with their forelimbs (see photo, page 21).

IN BRIEF **Class:** *Arachnids* **Order:** *Spiders* **Suborder:** *Tarantulas and relatives* **Family:** *Tarantulas* **Range:** *Myanmar, Cambodia, and Thailand*

Tiger Salamander

Ambystoma tigrinum

Characteristics: Depending on sub-species, TL up to 13¼ inches (33 cm), SVL 4¾–7¼ inches (12–16 cm). Males usually have longer tails, triangular in cross section. Cloaca swollen during mating season.

Terrarium type: ⌒
Level of difficulty: 1
Activity: ☀ ☽
Habit: ⚏ ○

Terrarium: Aquatic terrarium, with ⅓ water portion and water level of 6 inches (15 cm). Create steeply sloping transition to land portion. Recommended terrarium size for housing an adult pair: 32 × 16 × 16 inches (80 × 40 × 40 cm), 68–71.5°F (20–22°C), at night a bit cooler. Atmospheric humidity 80–100%. Lighting: 12–14 hours.

Keeping/Care: Keep animals of the same size as a group. You need to know their origin in order to provide appropriate temperature and hibernation conditions. Hibernation for northern subspecies 8–10 weeks at 35.5–41°F (2–5°C); for southern subspecies at 50–53.5°F (10–12°C). Reduce lighting period by 50%.

Diet: Insects, worms, slugs; pieces of fish also accepted.

Behavior: In their natural habitat, they live under leaves, wood, and stones, as well as in holes in the ground dug by mammals. Some forms are neotenic and must be kept in an aquarium.

IN BRIEF **Class:** *Amphibians* **Order:** *Salamanders*
Suborder: *Salamanders and their allies* **Family:** *Mole salamanders* **Range:** *Southern Canada to northern Mexico*

Timor Monitor Lizard

Varanus timorensis

Terrarium type:
Level of difficulty: 2
Activity:
Habit:

Characteristics: TL 24 inches (60 cm), SVL up to 8¾ inches (22 cm). Males have bigger heads and thickened tail bases.

Terrarium: Woodland terrarium with lots of climbing branches and hiding places. Plant with stiff-leaved species. Substrate: mixture of sand with forest humus and peat, 5½–8 inches (14–20 cm) deep. Supply fairly large water pan. Recommended terrarium size for housing an adult pair: 48 × 32 × 40 inches (120 × 80 × 100 cm). Temperature 82.5–86°F (28–30°C), at night 68–77°F (20–25°C), basking islands 95°F (35°C). Atmospheric humidity 60–90%. Lighting: 14 hours. UV radiation required.

Keeping/Care: Keep as a pair. Hibernation not required, but will stimulate reproduction. This species is one of the smaller members of its family and thus can easily be kept in a terrarium.

Diet: Large insects and small mammals, as well as fish.

Behavior: In the wild, lives on trees near bodies of water, leaving them only to hunt insects, mice, smaller reptiles, and amphibians.

IN BRIEF **Class:** *Reptiles* **Order:** *Scaled reptiles*
Suborder: *Lizards* **Family:** *Monitor lizards* **Range:** *Timor, New Guinea, Samoa, Savu, and Rotti*

Tokay Gecko

Gekko gecko

Characteristics: TL up to 14½ inches (36 cm), SVL up to 7¼ inches (18 cm). Males bigger, with larger preanal pores (see page 27).

Terrarium type:

Level of difficulty: 1

Activity:

Habit:

Terrarium: Woodland terrarium. Substrate: sand or mixture of sand and forest soil, 2 inches (5 cm) deep. Provide places for climbing and hiding. Recommended terrarium size for housing an adult pair: 44 × 44 × 60 inches (110 × 110 × 150 cm). Add 15% to area for each additional female. Temperature 81–91.5°F (27–33°C), at night 70–73.5°F (21–23°C), basking islands 104°F (40°C). Atmospheric humidity 50–70%, at night 80–90%. Lighting: 10–12 hours.

Keeping/Care: Keep as a pair or as a group with only one male. Because the species calls at night, don't place the terrarium near your bedroom.

Diet: Insects such as house crickets, cockroaches, field crickets, and grasshoppers. Baby, almost hairless, mice, and rats.

Behavior: These geckos are quick to defend themselves and have powerful bites. Handle them only if necessary and then only with gloves.

IN BRIEF **Class:** *Reptiles* **Order:** *Scaled reptiles* **Suborder:** *Lizards* **Family:** *Geckos* **Range:** *Northern India to southern China, as well as islands between Australia and Asia*

Tomato Frog

Dyscophus guineti

Also: Discophus guineti
Characteristics: SVL 4 inches (10 cm).
Males stay about ⅕ smaller.
Terrarium: Aquatic terrarium with ⅓

Terrarium type: 〰
Level of difficulty: 2 !
Activity: ☼ ☀
Habit: 🔲 ⬡

water portion and water level of 4–6 inches (10–15 cm). Substrate of land portion: peat, loam, and sand, 4¾–6¾ inches (12–17 cm) deep, kept damp enough for the frogs to burrow into in the daytime. Provide hiding places under roots or pieces of cork. Recommended terrarium size for housing up to 6 adults: 40 × 16 × 16 inches (100 × 40 × 40 cm). Temperature 73.5–82.5°F (23–28°C), at night 68°F (20°C), water temperature 77°F (25°C). Atmospheric humidity 80–100%. Lighting: 10–12 hours.
Keeping/Care: These frogs get along well together. Frequent water changes necessary. Caution: They have a skin secretion that causes swelling if you handle them. Wear gloves when working on the terrarium.
Diet: House crickets, field crickets, grasshoppers, and pinkie mice.
Behavior: Diurnal and crepuscular, but buries itself in the ground. Once well adapted, it can be observed in the daytime as well.

IN BRIEF   **Class:** *Amphibians* **Order:** *Frogs and toads*
Suborder: *Modern or advanced frogs* **Family:** *Narrowmouth or microhylid frogs* **Range:** *Southern Madagascar*

233

Tropical Girdled Lizard

Cordylus tropidosternum

Terrarium type: 🌵
Level of difficulty: 1
Activity: ☀
Habit: 🔅

Characteristics: TL 7¼ inches (18 cm), SVL 3¼ inches (8 cm). Males very slightly larger, with larger femoral pores (see page 26).

Terrarium: Steppe terrarium with plenty of places to hide and retreat under wooden roots and flat stones or in hollow trunks or cork tubes. Cover rear wall with cork. Substrate: 1¼–1⅜ inches (3–4 cm) of soil, loam, and sand, kept slightly damp only in the bottom-most layer. Supply water dish for drinking and bathing. Recommended terrarium size for housing an adult pair: 24 × 12 × 16 inches (60 × 30 × 40 cm). Temperature 86–95°F (30–35°C), at night 68–71.5°F (20–22°C), basking islands up to 104°F (40°C). Atmospheric humidity 40–60%. Lighting: up to 14 hours. UV radiation required.

Keeping/Care: These lizards get along well together. To stimulate breeding: hibernation for 6–8 weeks at 68–71.5°F (20–22°C), lowered by about 14°F (8°C) at night.

Diet: House crickets, field crickets, grasshoppers, cockroaches, *Zophobas* larvae, mealworms, wax moths and their larvae. Gut-load insects before feeding.

Behavior: Terrestrial, but also fond of climbing.

IN BRIEF **Class:** *Reptiles* **Order:** *Scaled reptiles*
Suborder: *Lizards* **Family:** *Spinytail or girdled lizards*
Range: *East Africa from Kenya to Zimbabwe*

Veiled Chameleon

Chamaeleo calyptratus

Characteristics: TL up to 24 inches (60 cm), SVL 10 inches (25 cm). Males easily identifiable by prominent tarsal spurs (thickenings on the hind legs) and larger head crests (casque).

Terrarium type: 🖼️
Level of difficulty: 2
Activity: ☼
Habit: 🌳

Terrarium: Woodland terrarium. Provide lots of horizontal branches for climbing. Important: large ventilation areas for fresh air. Advisable to use plants such as *Ficus benjamina*. Recommended terrarium size for one adult: 50 × 30 × 80 inches (125 × 75 × 200 cm). Temperature 82.5–90°F (28–32°C), at night 64.5–77°F (18–25°C), basking islands 95°F (35°C). Atmospheric humidity 50–70%. Lighting: 12–14 hours. UV radiation required.

Keeping/Care: Keep specimens singly; only place a pair together temporarily to attempt breeding. Mist terrarium daily to supply water. If a specimen refuses to eat, lack of water may be the cause. A drip system is highly recommended.

Diet: Field crickets, house crickets, cockroaches, grasshoppers, and baby rodents; leaves as well. Provide mineral supplements or gut-load insects prior to feeding.

Behavior: They become quite friendly toward their keepers.

IN BRIEF   **Class:** *Reptiles* **Order:** *Scaled reptiles*
Suborder: *Lizards* **Family:** *Chameleons* **Range:** *Yemen and southern Saudi Arabia*

Vietnamese Leopard Gecko

Goniurosaurus araneus

Also: Chinese tiger gecko

Characteristics: TL 7¼ inches (18 cm), SVL 4½ inches (11 cm). Males have clearly protruding hemipenal sacs (see page 26).

Terrarium type:

Level of difficulty: 2

Activity:

Habit:

Terrarium: Rainforest terrarium with substrate of sandy soil, 2 inches (5 cm) deep, kept slightly moist. Cover rear and side walls with coarse cork; at night the geckos can run around on this surface. Place flat pieces of cork on the ground as daytime hiding places. Plants serve as a screen and improve the terrarium microclimate. Recommended terrarium size for housing an adult pair: 24 × 16 × 20 inches (60 × 40 × 50 cm). Temperature 77–82.5°F (25–28°C), at night 61–68°F (16–20°C), in some places 90°F (32°C). Atmospheric humidity 70–80%. Lighting: 10–12 hours.

Keeping/Care: Keep as a pair or as a group with only one male. Hibernation: 10–12 weeks at 64.5–68°F (18–20°C), at night a bit cooler.

Diet: Field crickets, house crickets, cockroaches, and wax moths.

Behavior: They almost always defecate in the same corner, which makes cleaning easier.

Similar needs: *Goniurosaurus luii*

IN BRIEF **Class:** *Reptiles* **Order:** *Scaled reptiles*
Suborder: *Lizards* **Family:** *Geckos* **Range:** *Vietnam*

Western Banded Gecko

Coleonyx variegatus

Characteristics: TL up to 5⅝ inches (14 cm), SVL 3¼ inches (8 cm). Males identifiable by ⅕-inch (1–mm) long spurs on either side of the tail base.

Terrarium type: 🌵
Level of difficulty: 1
Activity: ☀ ☾
Habit: ⛰

Terrarium: Desert terrarium. Mixture of sand and loam as substrate, suitable for digging. Provide each animal with its own hiding place 3¼–4 inches (8–10 cm) high. Recommended terrarium size for housing an adult pair: 24 × 16 × 16 inches (60 × 40 × 40 cm). Increase area by 15% for each additional female. Temperature 81–90°F (27–32°C), at night 68–71.5°F (20–22°C), basking islands to 95°F (35°C). Atmospheric humidity 40–50%. Lighting: 12–14 hours.

Keeping/Care: Keep as a pair or as a group with one male. Hibernation: 10–12 weeks at 64.5–71.5°F (18–22°C) in the daytime and 53.5–59°F (12–15°C) at night, with lighting period of 6–8 hours.

Diet: Insects such as house crickets, cockroaches, field crickets, and grasshoppers.

Behavior: Though ground dwellers, they can climb quite well if the surface is rough enough.

Similar needs: Texas banded gecko (*Coleonyx brevis*)

IN BRIEF **Class:** *Reptiles* **Order:** *Scaled reptiles* **Suborder:** *Lizards* **Family:** *Geckos* **Range:** *Southwestern United States and northwestern Mexico*

Western Hognose Snake

Heterodon nasicus

Characteristics: TL 28 inches (70 cm), rarely up to 36 inches (90 cm). To ascertain sex, see page 15. Females larger.

Terrarium type: 🌵
Level of difficulty: 2 !
Activity: ☼
Habit: ⬚

Terrarium: Woodland or savannah terrarium with sandy substrate 4–6 inches (10–15 cm) deep (for burrowing). Supply small bathing pan. Decorate with roots, flat stones, pieces of bark, and low climbing branches. Plant with grasses. Recommended terrarium size for an adult pair: 28 × 14 × 14 inches (70 × 35 × 35 cm). Air temperature 77–81°F (25–27°C), at night 64.5–71.5°F (18–22°C), basking islands up to 90°F (32°C). Atmospheric humidity 50%. Lighting: 10–12 hours, partly UV.

Keeping/Care: These snakes get along well together. Hibernation: 12 weeks at 46.5–50°F (8–10°C).

Diet: Mice, pinkie rats, and toads.

Behavior: Predominantly diurnal, in their range of distribution also crepuscular and nocturnal at high temperatures. Newly caught specimens hiss, pretend to bite, and then play dead to defend themselves.

IN BRIEF **Class:** *Reptiles* **Order:** *Scaled reptiles* **Suborder:** *Snakes* **Family:** *Colubrids* **Range:** *Southern Canada to northern Mexico* **Important:** *These snakes engage in a bluff display when threatened but virtually never actually bite.*

White-headed Dwarf Gecko

Lygodactylus picturatus

Characteristics: TL 3⅝ inches (9 cm), SVL 1⅞ inches (4.5 cm). Males' rich yellow heads and shoulders contrast with their blue-gray bodies. Males of inferior status, like females, are plain brown.

Terrarium type: 🏔️
Level of difficulty: 3
Activity: ☀️ 🌅
Habit: 🌳

Terrarium: Woodland terrarium with cork rear wall for climbing, as well as climbing branches. Substrate: mixture of soil and sand. Provide hiding places among creepers and large-leaved green plants. Recommended terrarium size for housing an adult pair: 16 × 16 × 20 inches (40 × 40 × 50 cm). Temperature 77–90°F (25–32°C), at night 64.5–71.5°F (18–22°C). Atmospheric humidity 60–80%. Lighting: 12–14 hours. Provide UV light source.

Keeping/Care: During the reproductive period, a tree trunk is inhabited by only one pair, so it is advisable to keep only a pair in the terrarium.

Diet: Small field crickets, house crickets, grasshoppers, and wax moths and their larvae. Occasionally, overripe bananas.

Behavior: Fond of climbing and basking.

IN BRIEF **Class:** *Reptiles* **Order:** *Scaled reptiles* **Suborder:** *Lizards* **Family:** *Geckos* **Range:** *Ethiopia to Mozambique, Zaire in the west and Tanzanian islands in the east.*

White's Tree Frog

Litoria caerulea

Also: Great green tree frog, dumpy tree frog, *Hyla caerulea*, *Pelodryas caerulea*

Terrarium type: 🌊
Level of difficulty: 1
Activity: ☀ 🌙
Habit: ⬇⬇

Characteristics: SVL up to 4 inches (10 cm). Female's throats whitish, male's yellowish. Males also have a vocal sac, visible as an area of loose skin on the dark throat.

Terrarium: Woodland terrarium with water bowl large enough for soaking. Decorate with sturdy, large-leaved plants. Provide hiding places. Recommended terrarium size for up to 3 adults: 20 × 20 × 20 inches (50 × 50 × 50 cm). Temperature 73.5–82.5°F (23–28°C), at night 68°F (20°C), water temperature 77°F (25°C). Do not keep too damp, but mist about twice weekly. Atmospheric humidity 60–70%, at night 75–90%. Lighting: 10–12 hours.

Keeping/Care: Animals of roughly the same size are very compatible. Protect them against sunlight and drafts.

Diet: House crickets, grasshoppers, worms, or pinkie mice. These insatiable animals get fat quickly.

Behavior: Sleeps in the daytime in shady spots.

IN BRIEF **Class:** *Amphibians* **Order:** *Frogs and toads* **Suborder:** *Modern or advanced frogs* **Family:** *New World tree frogs* **Range:** *Rainforests and drier habitats of northeastern Australia and of southern Papua-New Guinea*

Whitetoe Tarantula

Avicularia metallica

Also: Metallic pinktoe tarantula

Characteristics: Body up to 2¹³⁄₁₆ inches (7 cm). See page 9 for sex determination.

Terrarium type: 🏞️
Level of difficulty: 1
Activity: ☀️ 🌙
Habit: 🌳

Terrarium: Moist woodland terrarium with substrate kept slightly damp. Provide cork tubes and cork rear wall. Supply shallow water dish. Recommended terrarium size for one adult: 12 × 12 × 16 inches (30 × 30 × 40 cm). Temperature 75–82.5°F (24–28°C), in places 86°F (30°C), at night 68–75°F (20–24°C). Atmospheric humidity 70–80%. Lighting: 8–10 hours.

Keeping/Care: Males and females can be kept as pairs for awhile, but they must be separated once the female has laid her eggs— 6–10 weeks after mating—if not sooner. Attach the lighting outside the terrarium, as the species likes to attach its silken retreats to lamps.

Diet: Flies, house crickets, grasshoppers, and young mammals.

Behavior: Peaceful species. When you work on the terrarium, these spiders will take fright easily and flee with lightning speed. Well-acclimated individuals can be placed on your palm without biting.

IN BRIEF **Class:** *Arachnids* **Order:** *Spiders* **Suborder:** *Tarantulas and relatives* **Family:** *Tarantulas* **Range:** *Guyana, Trinidad, Surinam, Ecuador, and northern Brazil*

Wood Turtle

Clemmys insculpta

Characteristics: CL about 9¼ inches (23 cm). Males have concave plastron (see page 26), bigger tails, longer toes on forelimbs.

Terrarium type:	
Level of difficulty: 1	
Activity:	
Habit:	

Terrarium: Woodland terrarium with substrate 6–8 inches (15–20 cm) deep and large bathing dish. Area (length × width) of at least 56 × 28 inches (140 × 70 cm) required for housing an adult pair. Air temperature 75–82.5°F (24–28°C), at night 61–64.5°F (16–18°C), water temperature 64.5–71.5°F (18–22°C), basking islands about 86°F (30°C). Lighting: up to 12 hours. UV radiation required. An outdoor pen year-round is ideal, but provide area of sandy or loamy soil so turtle can dig its hibernating burrow.

Keeping/Care: Keep as a pair or, after compatibility test, as a group with several females. Hibernation: up to 6 months.

Diet: Snails, earthworms, pinkie mice, strips of fish, dry food for aquatic turtles, fruits, and berries. Mineral supplementation advisable.

Behavior: These turtles are good climbers, so make sure the out-door pen is escape-proof. An intelligent and responsive turtle.

IN BRIEF **Class:** *Reptiles* **Order:** *Tortoises and turtles* **Suborder:** *Common-necked or straight-necked turtles* **Family:** *Pond and box turtles* **Range:** *Southeastern Canada to eastern United States. Protected over most of its range.*

Yellow Anaconda

Eunectes notaeus

Characteristics: TL 80 inches (200 cm), rarely up to 140 inches (350 cm). To ascertain sex, see page 15.

Terrarium type: 🌿
Level of difficulty: 3
Activity: ☀️ 🌅
Habit: 〰️

Terrarium: Rainforest terrarium with firmly anchored branches for climbing. Water pan at least 50% of the area. Recommended terrarium size for one adult: 80 × 40 × 80 inches (200 × 100 × 200 cm). Air temperature 77–86°F (25–30°C), at night 68–71.5°F (20–22°C), water temperature 77°F (25°C), basking islands 95°F (35°C). Atmospheric humidity 70–80%. Lighting: 12–14 hours, partly UV.

Keeping/Care: Advisable to keep singly because of cannibalism, as well as for safety. Hibernation: 3 months at 68°F (20°C), at night 59°F (15°C).

Diet: Rats, guinea pigs, rabbits, chicks, and doves. Some individuals reject certain types of food, while others eat those same types exclusively.

Behavior: Good climber, swimmer, and diver. Likes to stay in water pan. Specimens have different personalities, but most are aggressive, defensive, and attack readily.

IN BRIEF   **Class:** *Reptiles* **Order:** *Scaled reptiles*
Suborder: *Snakes* **Family:** *Boas and pythons*
Range: *Southern Brazil to northern Argentina*

Yellow-spotted Night Lizard

Lepidophyma flavimaculata

Characteristics: TL 6 inches (15 cm), SVL up to 2½ inches (6 cm). Hard to sex. Sex can be reliably ascertained only by endoscopy performed by a veterinarian.

Terrarium type: 🗾🗾
Level of difficulty: 1
Activity: ☽
Habit: 🌱🌱

Terrarium: Planted rainforest terrarium with climbing branches and hiding places under roots and pieces of bark on the ground. Provide place to bathe. Recommended terrarium size for housing an adult pair: 24 × 16 × 16 inches (60 × 40 × 40 cm). Temperature 71.5–82.5°F (22–28°C), at night 64.5–71.5°F (18–22°C), basking islands 95°F (35°C). Atmospheric humidity 70–90%. Lighting: 10–12 hours.

Keeping/Care: Keeping a pair is advisable, but males are relatively hard to obtain. (Note: This is now a separate species.) A very secretive species that is rarely observed even in the wild.

Diet: Small house crickets, field crickets, and grasshoppers.

Behavior: Reclusive, secretive, and difficult to observe. Crepuscular. The species is live-bearing and can reproduce without males (parthenogenesis).

IN BRIEF Class: *Reptiles* **Order:** *Scaled reptiles*
Suborder: *Lizards* **Family:** *Night lizards* **Range:** *Lowlands of northeastern Mexico to Panama*

Yellow-throated Plated Lizard

Gerrhosaurus flavigularis

Terrarium type: 🌵
Level of difficulty: 1
Activity: ☼
Habit: 🔱

Characteristics: TL 17 inches (45 cm), SVL 6 inches (15 cm). Males have yellowish throats and distinct femoral pores (see page 26).

Terrarium: Savannah terrarium. Loam and sand substrate, at least 6–8 inches (15–20 cm) deep. Include robust plants in pots. Provide stone slabs in a pile, roots, and branches that the animals can use for climbing and hiding. Provide large water container. Recommended terrarium size for housing an adult pair: 72 × 24 × 24 inches (180 × 60 × 60 cm). Temperature 86°F (30°C), at night 68°F (20°C), basking islands up to 104°F (40°C). Atmospheric humidity 50–60%. Lighting: up to 14 hours. UV radiation required.

Keeping/Care: Keep as a pair or as a group with one male. Can be kept outdoors in summer at high temperatures. For breeding: 4–6 weeks of hibernation at 61–68°F (16–20°C).

Diet: Field crickets, house crickets, grasshoppers, cockroaches, baby rodents, and occasionally fruit.

Behavior: Quite agile and fond of digging.

Similar needs: Black-lined plated lizard (*Gerrhosaurus nigrolineatus*)

IN BRIEF **Class:** *Reptiles* **Order:** *Scaled reptiles*
Suborder: *Lizards* **Family:** *Spinytail or girdled lizards*
Range: *Eastern Africa from Ethiopia to South Africa*

Index of Common Names

Page numbers in **boldface** refer to photos.

Index of Scientific Names

Page numbers in **boldface** refer to photos.

Subject Index

Page numbers in **boldface** refer to photos.